BAJA CALIFORNIA DIVER'S GUIDE

By
Michael B. Farley
and
Lauren K. Farley

First Printing, August 1984
Second Printing, February 1987
ISBN 0-932248-05-5
Library of Congress Catalog Card Number 84-060184
Cover Design andBook Illustrations: James Graca
Front Cover Photos:
    Michael Farley-(Sunset photo, Diver/Sea Fans)
    Howard Hall-(Manta Ray, Clarion Angelfish)
Back Cover Photo: James Graca
All photographs taken by the authors,
except where otherwise credited.
MARCOR PUBLISHING, PO BOX 1072, Port Hueneme, CA 93041

Table of Contents

Index of Maps

Introduction

The **Baja California Diver's Guide** is a fully revised and expanded edition of the first underwater guidebook to Baja California, entitled: "Diving Mexico's Baja California". First published in 1978, the original edition reflected the pioneering research of its authors, Michael and Lauren Farley. Over a period of several years, they explored and charted out much of the Baja California coastline, often camping on desert islands for extended periods of time, living with shark fishermen along the coast, and diving with native commercial divers.

Since the publication of their first edition, the authors have logged literally hundreds of additional hours underwater exploring and photographing Baja's vast marine wilderness. They have been able to share their in-depth knowledge of Baja's marine environment with sportdivers from all over the world through sportdiving, whale-watching, and filming expeditions to all parts of the peninsula. This thoroughly revised and updated edition not only contains a wealth of new diving sites and information, but also reflects the authors' unique, first-hand experiences as well as their sensitive appreciation of Baja California's underwater world.

The new **Baja California Diver's Guide** provides information on the nature of Baja's marine environment, tourist and diving facilities, weather and water conditions, and actual diving locations. As sportdivers are well aware, water and weather conditions can fluctuate greatly from one year to the next, and marine environments are in constant states of activity and change. In the case of Baja, hurricanes can greatly alter shoreline configuration from one year to another. The observations and facts set forth in this volume are the result of personal observations and opinions, as well as information compiled from a variety of reliable sources. This book is designed to provide a practical and enjoyable guide to Baja California's ocean world.

Foreword

The Baja California peninsula possesses over 3,000 miles of uninterrupted coastline sandwiched between two large bodies of water, the Pacific Ocean and the Sea of Cortez. Its coastal waters offer a spectacular variety of marine environments, from giant Pacific Ocean kelp beds to semi-tropical coral gardens and exciting underwater pinnacles and seamounts. Its foremost attraction, the Sea of Cortez, is known for its amazing variety and abundance of marine life, and has been the setting for incredible encounters between divers and giant manta rays, mammoth whale sharks, and schooling hammerhead sharks.

Although tourist development has slowly expanded throughout the peninsula, Baja California still remains a primitive wilderness paradise. It is a land of great contrasts, and for those of us fortunate enough to journey into its underwater world, nowhere does this contrast appear more dramatic than beneath the surface of its waters. Baja's rugged coastline and desert islands appear desolate and barren; yet their tidal shelves give way to rich and colorful reefs teeming with marine life.

Baja's marine wilderness holds an irresistible lure that compels one to return again and again to seek out its pristine harmony. As sportdivers, we share the rare privilege of observing firsthand a part of our planet that most people only glimpse in books or on television. We are able to interact with the marine environment, to observe the curious behavior of its inhabitants, to share exciting new discoveries, and to renew our spirits in its peaceful, fluid world. The Baja California Diver's Guide was written in the hope that it will give everyone who visits the Baja peninsula a greater appreciation and understanding of its marine environment, and that it may instill in its readers the desire to help protect and preserve it for future generations.

Acknowledgements

The authors wish to express their appreciation to Baja Expeditions Inc. for providing numerous opportunities for research and exploration in the Sea of Cortez aboard their fine charter dive boat, the *Don Jose*. The authors would also like to thank the Mexican Department of Tourism and FONATUR (Fondo Nacional de Fomento al Turismo) for their support in the completion of this publication, and for their continuing interest in promoting sportdiving activities in Mexico. The authors owe a great debt of gratitude to many people too numerous to mention who, over the years, have contributed support and information to the authors' underwater research in Baja California. A special thanks to Ricardo Perez Razura, Ricardo Garcia Soto, Luis and Leticia Klein, Enriqueta Velarde and T.W. and Joy Koskella. Finally, a gracious thanks to all of the people of Baja California whose lives are linked with the sea....to all of our fishermen friends and families who have guided us to innumerable new diving reefs, fishing banks, shipwrecks, seamounts and whale sharks. An important part of this book is a reflection of their wisdom and local knowledge, and their tales of the sea, which they have so generously passed on to us.

Tourist Information

Crossing the border into Mexico is a relatively easy procedure if you are informed of the latest regulations and are in possession of the necessary documents. All entry documents into Mexico are free, although personnel at some ports of entry may suggest a tip for facilitating your entry. Changes in immigration and custom regulations occur occasionally, so it is best to check with your travel agent, automobile club or the nearest Mexican government tourist office to obtain information on any new regulations that may be in force. Mexican government tourism office may be contacted at the following locations in the United States and Canada:

CHICAGO, ILL.	23 N. Michigan Ave. 60611
DALLAS, TEX.	Two Turtle Creek Village 75219
DENVER, COLO.	425 S. Cherry 80202
LOS ANGELES, CA	9701 Wilshire Blvd. 90212
MIAMI, FLA.	100 N. Biscayne Blvd. Tower Bldg. 33132
NEW YORK, N.Y.	405 Park Ave. 10022
SAN FRANCISCO, CA.	50 California Street 94111
TUCSON, ARIZ.	5151 E. Broadway 85711
WASHINGTON, D.C.	11 15th St. N.W. 20005
MONTREAL, QUE.	1 Place Ville Marie H3B 3M9
TORONTO, ONT.	101 Richmond St. West M5H 2E1
VANCOUVER, B.C.	700 W. Georgie St. V7Y 1B6

TOURIST CARDS

You will need to obtain a Mexican tourist card (TARJETA DE TURISTA) in order to travel in Baja California. The only exception to this is at the border towns and in the town of Ensenada, where you are allowed to visit for up to 72 hours without obtaining a tourist card. However, personal identification is still required.

There are two types of Mexican tourist cards available. Both are free of charge and are easy to obtain upon satisfactory presentation of proof of citizenship.

SINGLE ENTRY TOURIST CARD is issued upon proof of citizenship, and is valid for a maximum period of 90 days within date of issuance.

MULTIPLE ENTRY TOURIST CARD is issued upon proof of citizenship, and permits unlimited entry into Mexico for a 180-day period. Two passport-type photographs are required to obtain this type of permit.

Either of these types of tourist cards may be obtained through Mexican Border Immigration Offices, at Mexican Tourist Offices or Consulates, or through travel agents, travel clubs or airline companies.

PROOF OF CITIZENSHIP

U.S. CITIZENS - Passports are not required for U.S. citizens entering Mexico, but some proof of citizenship is required to obtain a tourist card. Any of the following documents will suffice as proof of citizenship: birth certificate (original or certified copy or notarized photostat of original or certified copy); a valid passport; notarized affidavit of citizenship; voter registration card or affidavit of registration; or military discharge papers. A U.S. driver's license is not recognized as proof of citizenship.

NATURALIZED CITIZENS - Naturalized citizens may present any of the following as proof of citizenship: an original certificate of naturalization; a valid U.S. passport; or the official plastic card issued by the U.S. Immigration and Naturalization Service.

CANADIAN CITIZENS - Canadian citizens must present one of the following for proof of citizenship in order to obtain a Mexican tourist card: a valid passport; or a birth certificate issued in Canada.

AUTOMOBILE REGULATIONS

If your driving itinerary does not take you outside the boundaries of the Baja California peninsula, a permit for your automobile is not required. However, it is always a good idea to carry your vehicle registration with you in case it should be required at check points by

Baja's Highway 1 is lined with miles of interesting desert scenery, such as this weird cirio tree.

authorities. When driving through mainland Mexico, or using the ferry boat services across the Sea of Cortez from Baja to the mainland, an automobile permit must be obtained.

Automobile permits are issued free of charge for a period of 90 days upon proof of automobile ownership (as well as proof of citizenship). Proof of car ownership may include: vehicle registration card; car title; or a notarized bill of sale. If the automobile is owned by a bank or finance company, or is registered in another person's or company's name, then a notarized letter from the lienholder or owner authorizing use of the vehicle in Mexico must be presented. Automobile permits are issued at all points of entry into Mexico and at all Baja California ferry ports.

INSURANCE - American automobile insurance policies are NOT valid in Mexico. For complete protection in Mexico, motorists should obtain a separate policy, covering both property damage and public liability. The cost of insurance is based upon the declared value of the vehicle and the length of time the automobile will be operated upon Mexican highways.

Mexican automobile insurance is issued by some U.S. insurance companies and automobile clubs, and through Mexican insurance companies which usually have offices near ports of entry into Mexico. Mexican insurance company offices are located at most major towns in Baja California, making it possible to obtain day-by-day coverage or to adjust the policy according to your travel needs.

TRAFFIC REGULATIONS

Generally, the maximum speed limit in Mexico is 100 kilometers (about 60 miles) per hour, or as otherwise posted. The limit is about 40 kilometers (25 miles) per hour in most towns and villages. Most cities and towns in Mexico have many one-way streets. Signs on each corner will usually indicate the traffic direction by an arrow, and two-way streets will have an arrow with two directions, or two points.

On the open highway, be extremely cautious of encountering livestock on the road, both during the day and at night. Respect the signs that indicate dangerous curves (CURVA PELIGROSA) on the highway, slowing down in anticipation of other vehicles. In Mexico, large trucks heavily laden with cargo often travel at snail-pace speeds. Usually, these truck drivers are courteous enough to signal cars behind them when it may or may not be safe to pass. If is is safe to pass, they will signal with their left blinker light for you to proceed; if it is not safe, they will signal with their right blinker for you to stay. Although this may not hold true in all cases, the majority of Mexican truck drivers use this system.

BAJA'S HIGHWAYS

Mexico's new transpeninsular Highway (Mex 1) is paved the entire length of its 1,000-mile stretch from Tijuana to Caba San Lucas. The road is a narrow, two-lane highway except for a brief four-lane span between Tijuana and Ensenada (on the Mex 1-D toll road). A general lack of shoulders on the highway, strong cross-winds in the valleys and plains, and steep grades in the mountainous areas require extra caution. Modern highway signs do give motorists advance warning of potential hazards. Driving at night is not recommended.

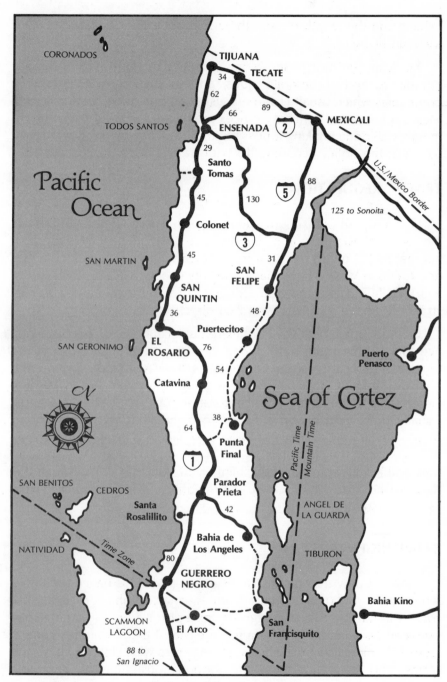

CORONADOS

TIJUANA

TECATE

34

62

66

89

ENSENADA

MEXICALI

TODOS SANTOS

2

29

U.S./Mexico Border

Santo
Tomas

Pacific
Ocean

45

130

5

88

125 to Sonoita

Colonet

3

45

31

SAN MARTIN

SAN
FELIPE

SAN
QUINTIN

36

48

Puertecitos

SAN GERONIMO

EL
ROSARIO

76

Puerto
Penasco

54

Catavina

Sea of Cortez

N

38

64

Punta
Final

1

Pacific Time

Mountain Time

Parador
Prieta

SAN BENITOS

CEDROS

42

ANGEL DE
LA GUARDA

Santa
Rosalillito

NATIVIDAD

Time Zone

Bahia de
Los Angeles

TIBURON

80

GUERRERO
NEGRO

Bahia Kino

SCAMMON
LAGOON

El Arco

San
Francisquito

88 to
San Ignacio

Baja California Norte

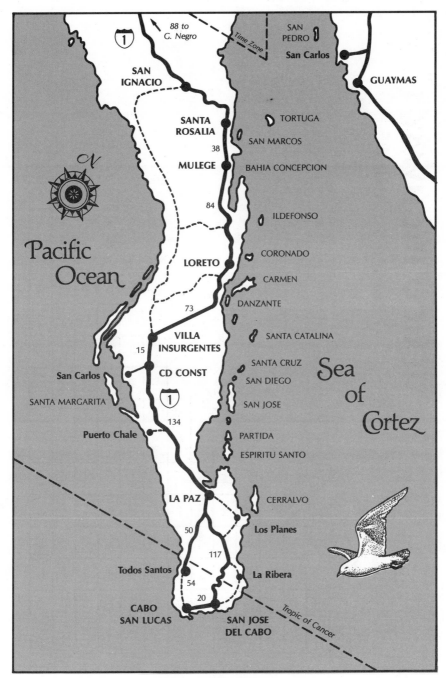

Baja California Sur

MEXICO HIGHWAY 1
Distance In Miles

To find the distance between towns, first find the northern town and read down the column. Second, find the southern town and read across the column to the left. The intersection of the two columns shows the distance between the two towns.

	Tijuana	Ensenada	Colonet	San Quintín	El Rosario	Cataviña	Parador Punta Prieta	Cuerrero Negro	San Ignacio	Santa Rosalia	Mulege	Loreto	Ciudad Constitución	La Paz
Ensenada	68													
Colonet	144	76												
San Quintín	187	119	43											
El Rosario	223	155	79	36										
Cataviña	299	231	155	112	76									
Parador Punta Prieta	364	296	220	177	141	65								
Cuerrero Negro	444	376	300	257	221	145	80							
San Ignacio	532	464	388	345	309	233	168	88						
Santa Rosalia	577	509	433	390	354	278	213	133	45					
Mulege	615	547	471	428	392	316	251	171	83	38				
Loreto	699	631	555	512	476	400	335	255	167	122	84			
Ciudad Constitución	788	720	644	601	565	489	424	344	256	211	173	89		
La Paz	922	854	778	735	699	623	558	478	390	345	307	223	134	
Cabo San Lucas	1059	991	915	872	836	760	695	615	527	482	444	360	271	137

A fleet of government-sponsored vehicles called the "GREEN ANGELS" regularly patrols the main highways, offering assistance to stranded motorists in emergencies. The English-speaking crews are prepared to aid in minor repairs, and carry extra supplies of gas, oil and water. Towing services can also be summoned. Their service is rendered free of charge, but motorists are charged the cost of any parts, gasoline or oil that they may require.

MEXICAN GASOLINE

When traveling along Baja's roadways, it is a wise idea to carry an extra 5-gallon container filled with fuel. Occasionally, gasoline stations run out of fuel and may not be able to dispense gas for several days due to delays from their suppliers. Also, even if you don't break down or need extra gas, you will always be able to help a fellow stranded motorist who has underestimated their gasoline needs. It is also wise to carry extra car parts such as fuel filters, fan belts, wheel bearings, hoses, water pumps, transmission fluid and engine oil. Because of the hot climate, multiple-grade oils and oils of 30-weight and less are not ordinarily used in Baja California. These grades are harder to find the farther south one travels.

PEMEX GASOLINE—The name PEMEX (Petroleos Mexicanos) refers to the gasoline stations which are conveniently located along Highway 1 and other paved or well-traveled routes in Mexico. They can be easily spotted along roadways, and are never more than 50 to 60 miles apart. Mexican gasoline stations may distribute three types of gasoline:

NOVA—dispensed from a blue pump as "regular" with an 81 octane rating.

EXTRA (unleaded)—dispensed from a silver pump as "extra", with a 92-octane rating.

DIESEL—dispensed from a red pump. Diesel fuel is widely available in Mexico, but it may not be found at all service stations. It is always wise to carry extra diesel fuel with you if your car uses diesel. When using diesel fuel in Mexico, an anti-bacterial agent should be added to prevent growth of sludge-causing bacteria in your tank. This is because diesel fuel only comes in one grade in Mexico and is of higher sulpher content than in the U.S.

FERRY SERVICE

Regularly scheduled ferry service connects Baja California with various points on mainland Mexico. These large, ocean-going vessels transport cars, trailer and boats, and provide accommodations for passengers. If you plan to take your vehicle from Baja California to the mainland you will need to obtain a car permit, which is available at all ferry ports. Fares for passengers are determined according to accommodations requested, which range from: SALON CLASS (reclining seats, no reservations), TOURIST CLASS (small room with bunk), CABIN CLASS (bedroom with bathroom), and SPECIAL CLASS (private suite, may not be offered on all ferries). Fares for vehicle are determined by length.

Santa Rosalia-Guaymas: Ferry service between Santa Rosalia and Guaymas currently operates 3 times weekly . . . on Tuesday, Thursday and Sunday. Eastbound ferries leave Santa Rosalia at 11 p.m., and arrive in Guaymas at 6 a.m.; westbound ferries depart Guaymas at 11 a.m. and arrive in Santa Rosalia at 6 p.m. The ferry office is located in the terminal building next to the harbor (phone in Santa Rosalia: (706) 852-0013, or 852-0014).

La Paz-Topolobampo: Ferry service leaves La Paz every Tuesday, Wednesday, Thursday (cargo only), Saturday and Monday, arriving in La Paz at 6 p.m. Reservations should be made at least 3 days in advance. The ferry office is located at Avenida Francisco I. Madero, 4 blocks east of the plaza (phone in La Paz: (706) 822-0109, or 822-2818).

La Paz-Mazatlan: Ferry service from La Paz to Mazatlan operates daily, departing at 5 p.m. The crossing takes 16 hours. Reservations should be made at least three days in advance (phone in La Paz: (706) 822-0109, or 822-2818).

Cabo San Lucas-Puerto Vallarta: Both eastbound and westbound ferries operate twice weekly, on Sunday and Wednesday from Cabo San Lucas, and on Saturday and Tuesday from Puerto Vallarta. Ferries depart from both ports at 4 p.m., and the crossing takes about 18 hours. The ferry office is located at the terminal on the south side of the harbor (phone in Cabo San Lucas: (706) 843-0079).

Happy passengers arriving at the international jetport in Loreto, one of Baja's major new tourist centers.

AIR SERVICE

There are presently four international jet ports in Baja California, located at the towns of TIJUANA, LORETO, LA PAZ and SAN JOSE DEL CABO, with flights connecting to various parts of the United States and other foreign countries. It is best to check with your travel agent regarding specific airline schedules. There are also domestic flights between major towns in Baja, and several airline companies periodically offer special charter services or irregularly scheduled passenger service to various destinations in Baja. Some of the major resorts in Baja also frequently schedule flights for their visitors with their own air transportation. Some of the major airline companies servicing Baja include:

AEROMEXICO: Offers nonstop flights between Los Angeles and Tijuana to La Paz and San Jose del Cabo. Flights also depart Tijuana and La Paz to a variety of Mainland Mexico cities.

MEXICANA: Offers nonstop service from Los Angeles to San Jose del Cabo and from Tijuana to La Paz, as well as flights to mainland Mexico from Tijuana, Mexicali and La Paz.

AIR CORTEZ: departs from Ontario Airport in Southern California, with twin-engine flights to Mulege and Loreto.

GUNNEL AVIATION: offers charter service from Southern California airports to a variety of destinations throughout Baja California.

BUS SERVICE

Bus service between major towns and cities in Baja is fairly regular and reliable. Regular bus service operates between Tijuana and La Paz through the Tres Estrellas de Oro bus lines. The trip takes about 30 hours. The American buslines, GREYHOUND and TRAILWAYS can ticket U.S. passengers to some of the major cities in Mexico, and can also provide schedule and fare information for the major Mexican buslines.

EQUIPMENT REMINDERS

Check your equipment carefully before traveling to Baja California, Make sure it is in good condition. Scuba diving shops in Baja California carry only a limited supply of equipment. Most of them carry very few spare parts. Some "extras" you may want to include in your gear include: extra straps, "O" rings, patching material, an extra knife, extra batteries for lights, and extra spear tips, rubber slings and fish hooks.

Do not venture into Baja's back regions unless you have adequate supplies of water, gasoline, food, and extra parts for minor auto repairs. Be prepared for small emergencies with a well-stocked first aid kit and a good first aid manual. You must be totally self-sufficient when exploring remote areas.

MEXICAN FISH AND GAME

A valid Mexican fishing license is required of any non-resident alien 12 years or older in order to fish from a private boat or from shore in Mexican waters. Each passenger aboard a private boat must possess a valid fishing license if there is fishing tackle present on board. Skin and Scuba divers must also possess a Mexican fishing license if they remove any type of sea life from Mexican waters, and especially if they are in possession of a speargun.

All fish and game regulations and limits applicable to sportfishermen in Mexico also apply to skin and scuba divers. Spearfishing is permitted only with a hand operated, spring and rubber powered spear gun. Catching, fishing or collecting of abalone, pismo clam, cabrilla, lobster, oysters, totoaba and turtles is forbidden. And the collection of any kind of coral or gorgonian is illegal. Sportdivers who confine their activities to sightseeing or photography do not need to obtain a fishing license.

Mexican fishing licenses are issued through the Mexican Fish Commission, the Mexican Tourist Department, and some Mexican insurance companies. Any motor-driven boat launched in Mexican waters also requires a permit. Boat permits and fishing licenses may be obtained from the following offices, either in person or by mail:

MEXICAN FISH COMMISSION
1010 2nd Ave, Suite #1605
San Diego, CA 92101
Phone #: 619-233-6956

MEXICAN FISH COMMISION
395 W. 6th Street, Rm#3
San Pedro, CA 90731
Phone #: 213-832-5628

EL PEZ MEXICAN SERVICE
406 S. Bayfront
Balboa Island, CA 92662
Phone #: 714-675-8200 or 714-675-5180

Before entering Mexico, it is your responsibility to check with the nearest office of the Mexican Fish Commission or Tourist Department to obtain the latest fish and game regulations. These, like other laws, are subject to periodic revision. As guests in Mexican waters, visiting sportdivers should comply with all existing regulations and practices. The Mexican Government Fish Commission also has offices in Tijuana, Ensenada, Mexicali and San Felipe in Baja California.

RECOMPRESSION CHAMBERS

There are some recompression chambers located throughout Baja California, but they are used primarily by local commercial diving cooperatives, and they may not be in operation year-round. Therefore, in case of a diving accident involving a decompression problem, the following emergency numbers may be used to summon medical aid:

1. Marine Radio Distress Frequency-Channel 1

2. U.S. COAST GUARD
   San Diego, California
   Emergency #: 619-295-3121

3. HYPERBARIC MEDICAL CENTER
   U.C.S.D. Medical Center
   LIFE FLIGHT EMERGENCY #: 619-294-3684
   (NOTE: This number may be used to summon emergency airlift aid in case of a diving decompression accident).

   RECOMPRESSION CHAMBER #: 619-294-52222

4. L.A. COUNTY U.S.C. Medical Center
   Recompression Chamber #: 213-221-4114

REMEMBER: PLAN YOUR DIVES AND DIVE YOUR PLAN. Use the Air Decompression Tables (with conservative margins for added safety) when planning deep or multiple dives with scuba equipment.

PHOTOGRAPHY EQUIPMENT

The submarine world of Baja California holds fascinating opportunities for the underwater photographer. Giant kelp forests, tropical coral gardens, and a super abundance of marine life varieties present challenging subjects for amateurs and professionals alike. The following items may be useful to keep in mind when planning a photo trip to Baja.

1. Bring your own film. Film sales are limited in Baja and stores which do carry film are likely to carry only black and white or color print film.

Baja's windswept beaches and intriguing lunar landscapes reward photographers with dramatic photos.

2. For battery-operated strobes, bring extra strobe batteries and store them in a cool place. For rechargable strobes, if you don't have your own generator, most hotels will allow you to use their electrical outlets. Also, there are ample recharging outlets on the charter dive boats in Baja for rechargable strobes.

3. Wait until you return home to have your film processed. Black and white processing with rapid development is available in larger towns in Baja, but color processing can take as long as a month.

4. Take special precautions to protect film and photo equipment from Baja's intense sun and heat while traveling. The fine dust on Baja's back roads can also damage unprotected equipment.

5. Don't forget to loosen the "O" rings that are used to seal underwater strobes, cameras and housings when traveling by plane.

6. Water visibility in both the Sea of Cortez and the Pacific Ocean fluctuate radically as a result of wind conditions, currents, tidal changes, plankton blooms, and ocean surge and swells. Be prepared with a wide-angle lens for days of poor water visibility.

The deserts, mountains and coastal regions of Baja California also reward photographers with unusual scenery and wildlife. Mangrove lagoons teem with exotic bird life. Offshore islands abound in sea lion rookeries. Unique flora and fauna thrive in desert terrain throughout the peninsula, and sculptured rock formations along the coastline cast intriguing shadows upon windswept beaches. The wonders of land and the sea combine to create a unique photographer's paradise in Baja's vast wilderness peninsula.

BAJA HOT LINE

To obtain the latest information on connecting ferry routes and schedules, as well as other tourist information in Baja, the BAJA INFORMATION SERVICE has been set up to provide up-to-date information for travelers at the following toll-free number: 1-800-522-1516

Chapter 1
Pacific Ocean: Northern Baja

Pacific Ocean: Northern Baja

Diving along Baja's Northern Pacific coastline primarily centers around the lively tourist town of Ensenada, located 60 miles south of the border. Ensenada is the only town on Baja California's Pacific coast that offers good facilities for visiting divers. Much of the diving along Baja's Pacific coast also originates from charter dive boats operating out of San Diego, with overnight and weekend trips to areas from the Coronados Islands to as far south as Sacramento Reef, or even the Cedros Island area. There are several offshore islands and submerged reefs and pinnacles all along the coastline that offer exciting diving opportunities, as many of these sites are seldom frequented by divers.

Most of Baja's Pacific Ocean coastline offers little in the way of good beach diving, however. A large part of the shoreline is either steep and inaccessible, or is occupied by long stretches of low-lying sand or cobblestone areas with heavy surf. A lack of good access roads into much of the coastal shoreline is also a limiting factor for beach diving. (The Punta Banda area outside Ensenada is one exception: beach diving is popular in several small coves around the point.) Generally, the best way to dive Baja's Pacific Coast is by chartering local boats and guides, or by launching your own boat at points along the coast, or from San Diego. Car-top boats and inflatables can also be launched over the beach at numerous points along the coast, and can be used to visit offshore islands, pinnacles and kelp beds.

PACIFIC OCEAN MARINE ENVIRONMENT

Baja California's Pacific Coast marine environment is characterized by an extremely diverse community of marine species, occupying a wide variety of underwater habitats. Marine environments along the coast range from long expanses of rocky open coastline, sandy open shores, bays and estuaries, deep submarine canyons, offshore islands, underwater sea cliffs and rock pinnacles, and lush kelp beds. The coastal waters of Northern Baja California are dotted with kelp beds, ranging from sparse stands to vast stretches of submarine forest. This wide variety of contrasting marine environments occuring in close proximity to each other offers a unique opportunity for an intermingling of marine species that would not ordinarily be found together.

The entire west coast of Baja California is generally considered to be an overlap zone between warm-water and cold-water species, containing numerous representatives of both the California temperate fauna and the tropical Panamic fauna. However, alternating areas of warm and cold water along the coast cause an uneven distribution of these warm and cold water species, rather than a gradual geographical transition. The cold southward-flowing California current, originating in the Gulf of Alaska, sweeps in along the Northern Baja coastline and creates isolated areas of cold water, as well as intense cold-water upwellings in certain locations, and especially around Cabo Colonet and Punta Banda. Marine life and submarine seascapes in these cold-water zones are reminiscent of Northern California (around Monterey and farther north), containing numerous species of fish and invertebrates that are either absent or poorly developed in nearby southern California.

South of San Quintin subtropical forms begin to appear in increasing abundance, and the large "Bahia Vizcaino" near Scammon's Lagoon is often considered to be the northern stronghold of much of the tropical Eastern Pacific fauna. But defining boundaries between the temperate and tropical species along the coast is arbitrary at best, with many exceptions that defy boundaries, such as the California Abalone which occurs all the way south to Cabo San Lucas.

Common fish species along the Northern Baja California coastline include: red snapper, sheephead, garibaldi, calico bass, several types of rockfish and kelp bass, perch, croaker, corbina, opaleye, cabezone, lingcod, halibut, barracuda, black sea bass, white sea bass, mackerel, and bonito, as well as varieties of blennies and gobies. Seasonal game fish, such as yellowtail and albacore, appear in the area from May through November. White sea bass are most abundant during the spring months.

The California spiny lobster (Panulirus) occurs along the entire Baja California west coast, as does the abalone (which is becoming somewhat scarce due to overharvesting). Other marine species include a variety of invertebrates, including anemones, nudibranchs, starfish, moray eels, sea urchins, sponges, gorgonian corals, hydrocoral, tunicates, rock scallops, mussels, crabs and other mollusks. The giant Pismo clam is abundant in the San Quintin area, and has been found as far north as Jatay Point in Baja.

Large colonies of sea lions, harbor seals and elephant seals inhabit offshore islands along the coast. A large variety of dolphins and cetaceans also roam the coastal waters, and the California Grey Whale can be seen traveling along the Northern Baja California coastline on its annual migrations from the Arctic to the warm lagoons of Baja from Vizcaino Bay southward to Madgalene Bay.

WEATHER AND WATER CONDITIONS

Water temperatures in Northern Baja California are cool enough to necessitate wearing a 1/4" wetsuit year-round. Winter water temperatures range from 50 to 56 degrees F, and summer surface water temperatures range from 56 to 75 degrees F; and from 48 to 64 degrees F below the thermocline. The months of August and September produce the warmest waters, and mid-summer through the late-fall months generally produce the best water conditions for diving. From January through late spring water visibility is adversely affected by plankton blooms, periodic storm activity and run-off from torrential rains

DECEMBER THROUGH FEBRUARY: Winds from the southeast and southwest frequently reach gale strength. Occasional storms produce heavy surge and wave action. Strong northerlies may also appear in periods of two to three days, and heavy winds reduce water visibility to below 20'. Diving conditions are generally poorest during these months. Heavy fog is frequent in the southern region.

MARCH THROUGH MAY: Prevailing winds from the northwest blow steadily, with only infrequent periods of calm. Winds are likely to increase greatly in strength in the afternoon. Water visibility averages 20' to 30', depending upon the duration of the prevailing winds. Diving conditions are usually better during the morning hours.

JUNE THROUGH AUGUST: Summer months produce lighter northwest winds, with more periods of intermittent calm and less ocean surge and wave action. Water visibility may fluctuate radically from 10' along some sections of the coast to more than 60' around offshore islands and pinnacle rocks. Occasional low-lying cloud banks and late-night and early-morning fog tend to keep daytime temperatures cool.

SEPTEMBER THROUGH NOVEMBER: Winds prevail from the northwest, but they are light and tend to allow more periods of calm weather than at any other season. Storms are generally infrequent and begin to make an appearance in late November. These months produce calm oceans and excellent sportdiving conditions. Water visibility is at its best, and often exceeds 100'.

Cold-water upwellings encourage the growth of giant anemones in Baja's Pacific waters.

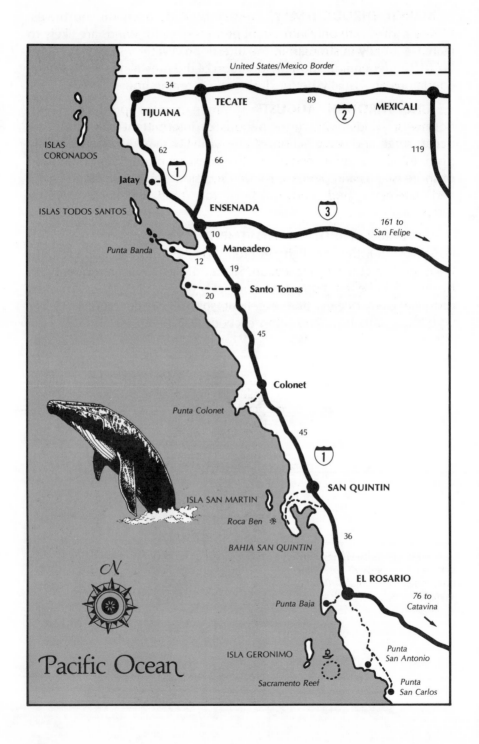

United States/Mexico Border

34

TIJUANA

TECATE

89

MEXICALI

2

ISLAS CORONADOS

62

1

66

119

Jatay

3

ISLAS TODOS SANTOS

ENSENADA

161 to San Felipe

10

Maneadero

Punta Banda

12

19

Santo Tomas

20

45

Colonet

Punta Colonet

45

1

SAN QUINTIN

ISLA SAN MARTIN

Roca Ben ✳

36

BAHIA SAN QUINTIN

N

EL ROSARIO

76 to Catavina

Punta Baja

Punta San Antonio

ISLA GERONIMO

Pacific Ocean

Sacramento Reef

Punta San Carlos

Los Coronados to El Rosario

Baja's Northern Pacific Coastline is a popular destination for sportboats and cruising yachts from southern California. Charter boats of all sizes radiate from resorts along the coastline, and many people trailer their own boats south along the modern paved highway which parallels the coast. Signs of rapid growth appear everywhere along the coastline of this region; but, at the same time, miles of rough dirt roads still lead into more remote regions where the sound of surf breaking on vast stretches of open shoreline beckon adventuresome travelers.

TOURIST FACILITIES

The close proximity of Baja's Northern Pacific coastline to Southern California draws hundreds of vacationers each year to its seaside recreational attractions. The major cities of Ensenada (which is an official port of entry into Mexico) and Tijuana are centers of modern commerce, development and tourism. They offer modern tourist accommodations and facilities, including hotels, campsites, RV and trailer parks, shopping markets, a wide range of restaurants and grocery stores, sporting and maritime events, nighttime entertainment, modern medical services (hospitals and pharmacies), and modern communication and transportation services.

BOAT LAUNCHING

Boat launching for trailered boats is available for a fee at the main harbor in Ensenada, with the use of a launching crane. Several resorts along the coast also have hard-packed ramps for small boat launching (although some are often periodically wiped out by storms and high tides). One popular small boat launching ramp near Ensenada is located at the La Jolla Beach Camp, on the southwest side of Todos Santos Bay. Good boat launching ramps are also available at tourist resorts located along the shores of San Quintin Bay.

Boats may be chartered through most of the resort hotels in the Ensenada area and south along the coast, and at the sportfishing pier in Ensenada. Small skiffs may be rented from local fishermen and commercial divers, who will also serve as guides. Small boats with guides may also be chartered through the local dive shops in the town of Ensenada. For group excursions into Northern Baja, several large charter boats also operate out of San Diego and offer good accommodations and reasonably-priced diving tours.

DIVING FACILITIES

The city of Ensenada hosts the only diving facilities along the entire Pacific Ocean coastline of Baja. There are two dive shops in Ensenada, both offering reliable air fills, equipment sales and rentals. Diving excursions can also be arranged through the shops. The dive shops are:

ALMAR DIVE SHOP
Av. Macheros #149
Ensenada, Baja California, Mexico

EL YAQUI DIVE SHOP
Blvd. Costero y Macheros
Ensenada, Baja California, Mexico

DIVING LOCATIONS

Ensenada Area

The coastline between Tijuana and Ensenada is a 60-mile expanse of open coastline, comprised of long stretches of sandy beaches, broken by occasional steep and perpendicular cliffs and small gravel beaches. Beach diving along this section of the coast is limited by lack of access due to rugged terrain, lack of roads and privately held land. Although there are some large, offshore kelp beds offering good diving, the coastline is exposed to surge and swells from all directions, and boats must be launched through the surf.

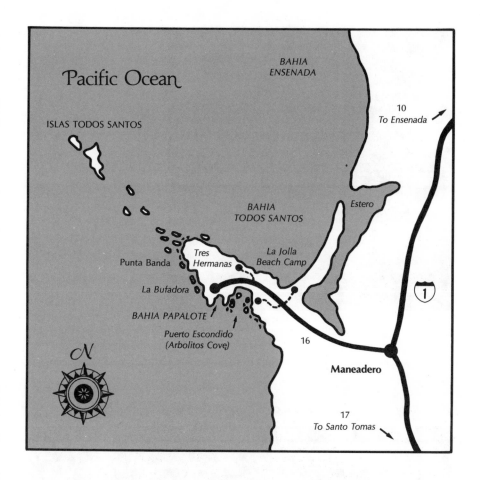

Pacific Ocean

ISLAS TODOS SANTOS

BAHIA ENSENADA

10
To Ensenada

BAHIA TODOS SANTOS

Estero

Tres Hermanas

Punta Banda

La Jolla Beach Camp

La Bufadora

BAHIA PAPALOTE

Puerto Escondido (Arbolitos Cove)

16

Maneadero

17
To Santo Tomas

N

Punta Banda Area

PUNTA BANDA forms the southern edge of the BAHIA TODOS SANTOS (Todos Santos Bay), the large bay back of which is situated the city of Ensenada. A good paved road forks right at Maneadero (10 miles south of Ensenada) and continues along the backbone ridge of Punta Banda a distance of 12 miles. The road ends at the village of La Bufadora located on the southwestern side of the point back of PAPALOTE BAY. Punta Banda is characterized by steep cliffs surrounded by numerous detached rocks, pinnacles and kelp beds. Several excellent diving locations, accessible by boat and from shore, are located along both sides of this ridge.

The California red lobster is abundant along Baja's Pacific Coastline.

The California Garibaldi is also a common reef-dweller in Baja's waters.

THE NORTH SIDE of Punta Banda comprises the area inside Todos Santos Bay from Camp La Jolla along the coast past Three Sisters Rocks (Roca Tres Hermanas) and continuing northward to the point itself. Steep cliffs with rough hiking trails leading to rocky beaches predominate. Beach entries are strenuous with scuba equipment, but many divers do negotiate the steep cliffs for both snorkeling and diving.

Although the north shore of Punta Banda fronts the sandy Todos Santos Bay, most of the beaches and the shallow subtidal areas are rocky. A narrow band of gently sloping rocky underwater terrain (comprised of rock, cobblestone and some large boulders), with depths ranging from 40' to 60', borders most of this shoreline. These rocky areas extend out from shore to distances of 100 to 200 feet before ending in a bottom comprised of fine sand. Kelp beds along this side of Punta Banda are sparce, and are generally not within comfortable swimming distance from shore with scuba equipment.

NORTHWEST TIP OF PUNTA BANDA marks one of the best diving locations around Punta Banda. It is accessible by boat only, and recommended for experienced divers, as heavy surge and open ocean conditions often prevail around the point. A long chain of islets extending 1½ miles from the point in a northwest direction marks a rich underwater ridge comprised of sheer rock walls, rock pinnacles, underwater cliffs, caves, crevices and sporadic kelp beds. The outermost group of rocky islets along this ridge is characterized by a navigation light atop one of them. Depths drop rapidly to 60' close around the rocky walls, sloping gradually to extreme depths.

This area contains some of the most colorful and abundant marine life in the Punta Banda area. The cold upwelled water along the south side of these islets provides a wealth of nutrients, encouraging luxurious kelp growth. Cold water temperatures also produce submarine seascapes reminiscent of Northern California, and promote good water visibilities.

Underwater cliffs and pinnacles are usually covered with colorful growths of sponges, mollusks and tunicates which are largely absent in the warmer bordering waters of southern California. Red algae, hydrocorals and sheets of fluorescent anemones cover many of the cliffs and pinnacles, splashing brilliant colors over the rocky surface. Thick beds of mussels line rock crevices, and lush beds of eel grass dominate the shallower portions.

SOUTH SIDE OF PUNTA BANDA is comprised of a maze of rock-bound inlets and small islands with occasional sand patches near shore. A rocky underwater shelf about 2,000 feet broad also extends out from the south side, dropping gradually to a sandy shelf about 130 feet below the surface. The south side is characterized by intense cold-water upwellings, producing very cold and generally clear water.

Underwater pinnacles are scattered all along this side, continuing into the center of PAPALOTE BAY. Small islets well offshore usually mark the top of a pinnacle. Isolated, roundish patches of kelp well out from shore may also indicate the location of an underwater pinnacle. Depths range from 30' along the rocky cliffs inshore to 60' to 100' along the outer edges of detached rocks and pinnacles. A large kelp bed is located across the entrance of the largest cove immediately south of the tip, and offers excellent diving conditions.

This area is accessible by boat, or may be accessed by very steep, rugged trails. The south side of Punta Banda is exposed to ocean swells, and surge along the cliffs can produce hazardous diving conditions in poor weather.

BAHIA PAPALOTE (PAPELOTE BAY) is the name of the large cove back of which lies the resort village of LA BUFADORA. The paved road along Punta Banda ends at the cove, and a dirt road provides access to a natural phenomenon called LA BUFADORA (The Blow Hole), which is a geyser-like spout of seawater that sprays upward as much as 100' into the air.

Underwater hot springs are also located inside Papalote Bay, as well as in the estuary along the north side. The hot water flow from these springs covers about half an acre at depths from 80 to 100 feet. Although the heat flow does not significantly affect water temperatures, the bottom is appreciably warmer and small streams of bubbles can be seen coming up through the sand.

Papalote Bay is one of the few coves in the area with easy access and beach entries to good diving locations. Colorful pinnacles lie within easy swimming distance from shore, and a large kelp bed is located along the northern side. Several large sea cliffs also line the edges of the cove. Depths average 40' to 60', and drop to over 100' on the outer edges of the kelp beds. LA BUFADORA is a good place to charter boats with local guides for diving excursions north and south along the shore of PUNTA BANDA.

The rocky pinnacles and cliffs at Arbolitos Cove typify the Punta Banda shoreline.

PUERTO ESCONDIDO (also known as ARBOLITOS COVE) is the largest cove just southward of PAPELOTE BAY. It is comprised of two bays which face southward and are separated by a rocky outcropping. A rough dirt road branches over the mountain from the paved road along PUNTA BANDA, at a point just north of Camp La Jolla.

This cove has a good landing beach for launching small boats, and easy beach access to the surrounding waters. Several large, detached rocks lie close along its steep shoreline and also toward the center of the cove, and scattered patches of kelp appear inside the cove.

Exploration by boat south of PUERTO ESCONDIDO reveals precipitous cliffs, with pinacle rocks awash and submerged amid beds of kelp. The area is not heavily frequented by sportdivers because of the difficult access road. When weather conditions from the south are favorable, both snorkeling and diving are excellent. Small skiffs can often be rented from the local fishermen who conduct fishing activity from the cove.

Islas Todos Santos

The Todos Santos Islands (All Saints Islands) are located approximately 3-1/4 miles northwest of PUNTA BANDA, and can be easily seen from Ensenada on a clear day. The islands are comprised of two large rocky masses of land surrounded by extensive beds of kelp and detached rocks, both submerged and awash.

The islands may be accessed by boat from Ensenada or Punta Banda. Several coves on the lee of the islands afford good protection from prevailing winds. The Todos Santos Islands are regularly visited by sportfishing boats from San Diego and Ensenada, and are known for their great abundance of game fish, especially yellowtail. The islands are an outstanding diving location, and are washed by cold-water currents that support rich concentrations of marine life and good water clarity.

THE WEST AND SOUTHWEST SIDE of the islands presents the best sportdiving locations, with greater concentrations of kelp beds and marine life. Depths range from 60' to 80' on the outer fringes of the kelp beds, with rocky reefs and pinnacles scattered over a sandy bottom. This side of the islands is exposed to cold-water upwellings, and is also open to wind conditions from the south and west. Surge around the reefs can be extremely rough when winds blow with any intensity.

THE PASSAGEWAY located between the two islands is generally shallow, with depths of 10' to 30' over clumps of detached rocks and thick growths of eel grass. Medium to strong wave action may stir up considerable sand in the channel, adversely affecting water clarity. During periods of calm, the passageway is a good free-diving spot.

THE SOUTHERN ISLAND is characterized on its eastern side by several deeply indented coves that provide good shelter for boats and which afford good sportdiving. Detached rock pinnacles lie close around the edges of the coves, and depths inside the cove vary from 20' to 40', and rapidly reach depths of 60'-plus seaward. Kelp patches are only sporadic, but the best all-weather diving is located around these coves. Often, while the rest of the islands are beset by surge, the coves on the southeastern end are calm and clear.

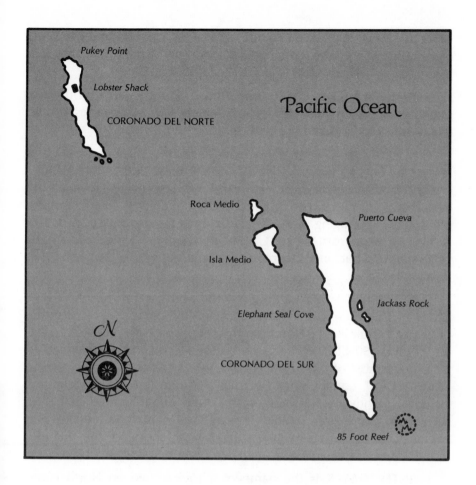

Pukey Point

Lobster Shack

CORONADO DEL NORTE

Pacific Ocean

Roca Medio

Puerto Cueva

Isla Medio

Jackass Rock

Elephant Seal Cove

N

CORONADO DEL SUR

85 Foot Reef

Los Islas Coronados

The Coronados Islands (Islas Coronados) comprise a group of four steep and rocky islands located seven miles offshore from the Baja peninsula, and 13 miles south of Point Loma near San Diego, California. The waters surrounding the island offer an unusual diversity of underwater terrain, from rocky ledges and pinnacles to lush kelp forests and sand and rock flats.

These islands are regularly visited by sportdiving boats from San Diego. These islands are extremely rich in marine life, and have long been a popular diving destination for California sportdivers. They are primarily known for their abundance of game fish, such as yellowtail, white sea bass, halibut, barracuda, calico bass, bonito and black sea bass. Lobster are also abundant around the islands, but they are protected by Mexican law and are illegal to take.

NORTH ISLAND is the northernmost of the island group and measures approximately one mile in length. Diving locations around this northernmost island are both exciting and diverse.

THE WESTERN SIDE of North Island faces out to open ocean and resembles one continuous cliff. Diving the west side of the island is only possible on calm days, with early morning diving providing the best chance of encountering good diving conditions. Depths inshore are shallow, averaging 20' to 30', but plunge rapidly to depths of 100' within 50 yards from shore. Game fish abound, including sea bass, yellowtail, halibut and sheephead. A large colony of sea lions also inhabits the area.

PUKEY POINT is the name given the northeastern tip of NORTH ISLAND. This dive site is characterized by vertical drop-offs that plummet in stair-like fashion from the shoreline, with drop-offs to 20', 40', 80' and 150'-plus. While sandy bottoms appear at depths of 60' to 80' around most of the CORONADOS, even the deep terrain around PUKEY POINT continues to be rocky. Marine life is abundant and includes brightly colored gorgonian corals, bright orange garibaldis, sheephead, cabezone, sculpin, lingcod, and numerous blennies and gobies. Schools of yellowtail appear near shore in the summer months, and schools of blacksmith can often be observed in the area.

LOBSTER SHACK is the name of a rocky cove on North Island located just south of PUKEY POINT. It is marked by a rickety wooden shack (called the lobster shack), and provides a good small boat anchorage and a good shallow diving location. A gradually sloping rock wall drops to depths of 30' to 50'. This cove is known for its unusually clear water, and fish photography is excellent. Fish in this shallow reef have been hand-fed by so many divers that such fish as garibaldi, opaleye, kelp bass and sheephead are likely to approach divers and beg for food. The same also holds true with the moray eels in the cove, which are also numerous and used to being fed by divers.

SOUTHWEST END of North Island is a challenging diving spot for the more advanced divers. The island narrows to an isthmus which is connected to the main island by a rock arch. Just north of the arch is a sand and rock shelf with depths averaging 50'. A cliff just south of the arch drops to over 110', its sheer walls and overhangs covered with brightly colored red and yellow anemones. Surge and currents frequently arise around the arch, so this site should only be visited when diving conditions are at their best.

MIDDLE ROCK AND MIDDLE ISLAND are the two small islands between North and South Coronado. MIDDLE ROCK is best known for its rock ledges which extend south and east from the small island continuing through the narrow slot that separates Middle Rock and Middle Island. Currents in the area can be quite strong and unpredictable, and the area has been nicknamed "Anchor Heaven," as ledges filled with abandoned anchors attest to its reputation as a treacherous anchorage. However, this 40' to 60' deep reef area between Middle Rock and Middle Island is an interesting dive site, noted especially for its abundance of soupfin sharks.

MOONLIGHT COVE is the name of a large cove that bisects Middle Island on its eastern side toward the southern end. The cove provides a good boat anchorage that is close to good diving sites. Reefs inshore drop to 30', and rock walls are covered with colorful nudibranchs, starfish and anemones. Kelp and sea grass grow along the sandy bottoms, but fish life is somewhat scarce. Colonies of harbor seals around Middle Coronado Island often swim with divers.

SOUTH ISLAND is the largest of the Coronados Islands, measuring 1-3/4 miles in length.

THE NORTH END of South Island is marked by a group of detached rocks which extend off the point in a northwesterly direction. This area is known for its rich abundance of sea life. Exceptionally large sheephead populate reefs along the seaward side, and garibaldi, sea bass, red snapper, halibut and yellowtail feed in the kelp beds along the shore.

SEAL COVE is located halfway down the weather side (western side) of South Island. This cove is noted as a sea lion rookery, and often elephant seals can be seen in the area. Weather and surge conditions can be very severe on the western side of the island, limiting diving in prevailing northwesterly wind conditions.

SOUTHEASTERN END of the island offers the most outstanding kelp diving to be found around the islands. A large, thick kelp bed lines the southeastern shore of South Island, where depths begin at 20', then gradually slope to 85', several hundred yards from the island. A great

Large beds of kelp flourish along Baja's Pacific Ocean coastline. (photo: Howard Hall)

variety of marine life flourish around these lush kelp beds, including schooling game fish, the usual reef fish and moray eels, and such oddities as large spider crabs and bat rays.

FIVE-MINUTE KELP BED is the name given a large area of kelp located south of the lighthouse (about five minutes by boat) on the southern tip of South Island. This area is known for its abundance of white sea bass, black sea bass and yellowtail.

EIGHT-FIVE FOOT REEF is located about 3/4 of a mile offshore, just east of the lighthouse on the southeastern end of the island. The reef is difficult to find and the use of a fathometer is a must. Depths vary from 60' to 85' over the reef, and the shallowest pinnacle of the reef rises to within 60' of the surface. Big game fish are abundant around the reef, and colorful invertebrate life make this an excellent photography site. Strong currents frequently arise in the area, and open ocean conditions prevail, so caution should be exercised.

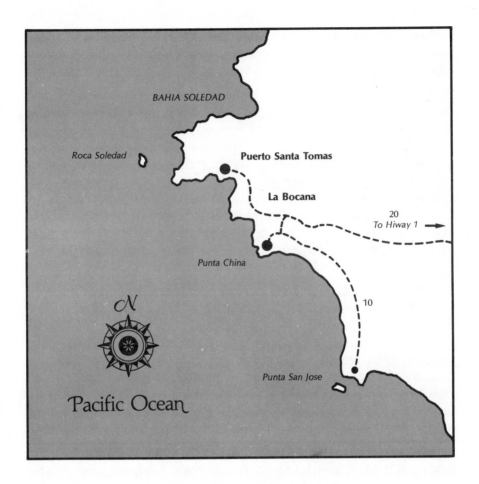

The following labels appear on the map:

BAHIA SOLEDAD

Roca Soledad

Puerto Santa Tomas

La Bocana

20
To Hiway 1 ➔

Punta China

10

N

Punta San Jose

Pacific Ocean

Santo Tomas Region

The junction into Santo Tomas and La Bocana branches off from the main highway 30 miles south of Ensenada, just north of the village of Santo Tomas. The road stretches 20 miles through the lush, fertile Santo Tomas Valley before reaching the coast. There are actually two roads that lead into the region. The old road crisscrosses the sandy stream bed along the floor of the valley, but sections of this road wash out very easily after rainstorms, leaving it impassable. Because of this, a new graded dirt and gravel road was recently completed into the region. The new road follows the contours of the northern wall of the steep, chaparral-covered hills high above the valley floor. The road is well-graded, but parts of the road are extremely steep, with sharp curves and grades, that would make towing a boat over this road very difficult.

There are no diving facilities in the region, and only minimal tourist facilities. Sprawled along the cliffs overlooking the water are several private residences and summer homes. There is a small fee for camping just back of the beach, and a small store where minimal grocery provisions and fresh water may be obtained. Rustic cabins with gas stoves are sometimes available for rent, and fiberglass skiffs can also be rented through the proprietor of the store. There is no boat launching ramp, but through-the-surf launching of small car-top boats and inflatables can be accomplished on calm days. Free diving is excellent along the rocky coast, but better diving locations to the kelp beds close off-shore are better accessed by boat.

BAHIA SOLEDAD is a large, shallow bay located just north of Punta Santo Tomas, just ten miles by sea south of Punta Banda. Depths are generally shallow within the bay (40′ and less) with a scattering of sand, rock, eel grass and sparce kelp patches. The detatched rocks surrounded by kelp at the points on either side of the bay provide the best diving locations, with depths averaging 60′ to 80′. Treacherous cliffs limit land access to the water, and the area is best accessed by boat. The bay is exposed to prevailing northwest and west winds, which often create large swells around the points and inside the bay.

ROCAS SOLEDAD REFERS TO A LARGE GROUP OF DETACHED ROCKS LOCATED west of Santo Tomas Point. Easily recognizable by their white covering of bird lime, the rocks are surrounded by occasional kelp patches and are exposed to all weather conditions. Depths slope from 40′ to well over 100′ on their seaward side, where sheer vertical drop-offs lined with large fissures and crevices house colorful invertebrate life and lobster.

PUERTO SANTO TOMAS comprises the large bay inside the point, backed by a small resort and fishing village. A landing place for small skiffs is located at the northern end of the cove. A large kelp bed lies across the entrance to the bay, with generally shallow depths prevailing (30′ to 50′). Outside the bay, several detached rocks, both awash and submerged, lie close off the point. The area is heavily fished by locals, and marine life is likely to be more abundant around the outermost rocks and points. Water visibility is usually poor inside the cove.

LA BOCANA is located at the southern end of Santo Tomas Bay. it is comprised of a sand beach behind which a small grocery market is located. Kelp beds line the entrance to the bay, with depths of 30' to 50' over scattered rock and sand areas. Easy water entries may be made from low-lying points along the rocky cliffs, but surge and currents often limit water visibility.

PUNTA CHINA is accessible by a dirt road branching south from la Bocana. A limestone quarry is located in the vicinity and a small fish camp occupies the point. Kelp beds continue offshore from Punta China to about one mile southward of the point. Sportdiving around the point itself is excellent, and the area is noted for its abundance of lobster and kelp fish.

San Quintin Area

The small town of San Quintin stretches haphazardly along the main highway for several miles. It is the center of an agricultural region, and most of the businesses along the main street of town, (which include stores and cafes, banks, gas stations, movie theaters, etc.) cater primarily to local residents.

The tourist attraction in this area is not the town itself, but rather lies along the shores of the large BAHIA DE SAN QUINTIN, located a couple of miles off the main highway. The bay is accessible by numerous roads that branch west from the highway leading to several tourist resorts situated along the shores of the bay. The San Quintin Bay is one of the most popular tourist destinations between Ensenada and Mulege.

Most people are drawn to the San Quintin Bay by the excellent fishing attractions in nearby waters and along scenic beaches. Camping areas, modern hotels and trailer parks are easy to find and several modern resorts offer boat charter services. The quiet waters of the inner bay provide a good sheltered harbor for small boat anchorage and launching. Trailered boats may be launched into San Quintin Bay at the military complex near the Old Mill Motel (MOLINO VIEJO). The bay is an excellent point of departure for sportdiving excursions to the waters around SAN MARTIN ISLAND, one of the most outstanding diving attractions in the area.

ISLA SAN MARTIN (San Martin Island) is a small round island, one mile in diameter, located just outside San Quintin Bay about 3 miles offshore. Large beds of kelp around the island, with numerous detached rocks and pinnacles, attract a good abundance of marine life. Depths close inshore around the island range from 30' and less on the leeward side, with more severe depths on the weather side reaching 60' to 90' at the outer edges of the kelp beds. The weather side (western side) is less protected from wind conditions, but the best sportdiving sites are located around this side of the island.

A small indentation on the eastern side of the island, called HASSLER'S COVE, provides good anchorage and protection for small craft in the area. The coastline north of the cove offers good diving conditions, with shallower depths along the shoreline and generally calm waters. Playful sea lions in the area often swim with divers. Fog may arise quickly around the island, so good compasses are a must for small boat navigation.

BEN'S ROCK (Roca Ben) is the name commonly given a submerged rocky pinnacle located about three miles south of San Martin Island. The rock rises to within 10' of the surface and plummets sharply to immediate depths of 80' and 100', close around its steep walls. The area is usually devoid of kelp, and cold waters promote good water visibilities. Open ocean conditions prevail, and this site is recommended for experienced divers. Several species of large game fish frequent these pinnacles seasonally.

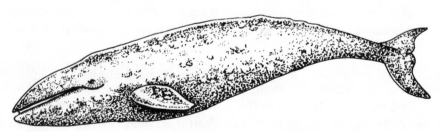

CALIFORNIA GREY WHALE
Eschrichtius glaucus

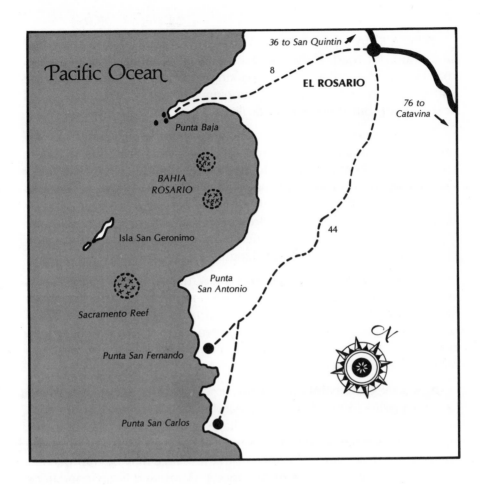

The map shows the coastline with labels: Pacific Ocean, 36 to San Quintin, 8, EL ROSARIO, 76 to Catavina, Punta Baja, BAHIA ROSARIO, Isla San Geronimo, 44, Punta San Antonio, Sacramento Reef, Punta San Fernando, Punta San Carlos.

El Rosario Region

The coastline south of the small town of El Rosario gives access to some of the most interesting and prolific waters on Baja's Northern Pacific coast. Large beds of kelp in Rosario Bay and around San Geronimo Island teem with marine life, and nearby Sacramento Reef is surrounded by the remains of dozens of shipwrecks.

Beach diving along the coast is limited by lack of access roads and rugged coastal terrain. A small, sheltered cove at Punta Baja is accessible by a dirt road leading into the region from El Rosario. Small skiffs and inflatables can be launched through the surf on calm days. Larger boats should be launched at San Quintin, 35 miles to the north.

PUNTA BAJA is located 12 miles southwest of El Rosario at the end of a good dirt road. Cartop and small trailered boats and inflatables may be launched off a concrete parking area near the beach when the surf is not too heavy. Primitive camping sites are located around this scenic point, but there are no facilities.

Large breakers rolling in around the point attract surfers to the area, but diving along the point is not recommended, due to heavy surge and swells that frequently break over the low-lying shoal rocks lying close around the point. Better sportdiving locations in the area can be found in the waters south of Punta Baja, and are accessible by boat only. Diving excursions from small boats can sometimes be arranged through local fishermen who frequently depart for San Geronimo Island from the launching area.

ROSARIO BAY is a large bay that measures 13 miles across between Punta Baja and Punta San Antonio. Several large kelp beds located within the bay provide homes for marine life and offer good diving locations, with depths ranging from 20' to 60'. While these kelp beds are easily reached by boat from Punta Baja, they are located too far offshore for beach diving.

ISLA SAN GERONIMO (San Geronimo Island) is a low lying island located 9 miles south of Punta Baja, and situated 5 miles offshore at its closest point. A seasonal fishing village is located on the southeast side, where a small cove provides the only protection from prevailing winds. Local divers and fishermen from the village may be approached for emergency gas supplies or provisions. Damp and foggy conditions are common year-round, and the island often appears as a large rock enshrouded in fog and gray clouds. There is a very picturesque lighthouse on the highest point of the island. Sportdiving around the island is excellent.

The best place to dive around the island is at the southeastern end. A reef of submerged rocks extends half a mile off the southern point in a southwesterly direction, and depths reach 90' on the outer edges of the reef. Extensive kelp beds surround the point, with depths ranging from 10' and less close inshore to 70' at its outer edges, over a rocky bottom full of interesting fissures and caves. Underwater pinnacles appear outside the kelp beds in depths of 80' to 90', and gardens of colorful sea fans grow profusely on the rocky surfaces. This is an outstanding place for both close-up and wide angle photography. Water visibility is best during the late summer and fall months.

Looking over San Geronimo Island towards Sacramento Reef, a navigational hazard that can be difficult to distinguish when seas are rough.

This small island is also a naturalist's paradise. Rocks off the southern end of the island are covered so thickly with sea lions that they appear to be blanketed with fur from a distance. At the northern end of the island, diving conditions are generally poor due to heavy surge and sparse kelp beds, but various species of marine birds that occupy a giant nesting ground back of the shore are interesting to observe.

SACRAMENTO REEF is located 1-1/2 miles southeast of San Geronimo Island. This rocky reef is steep and almost totally submerged. It measures 2-1/4 miles long and 1-1/4 mile wide. The reef has been termed the "Graveyard of the Pacific," as many a ship has floundered on its concealed rocks over the years. Parts from shipwrecks lie strewn over the backbone of the reef. Years of wave action and winds have scattered them in all directions, and heavy growths of eel grass and kelp camouflage most of the remains of old shipwrecks.

The reef can be easily located on a calm day by the breakers awash over the top of the reef at a point about 5 miles directly west of San Antonio Point. Shallow depths around the partially submerged rocks drop rapidly to depths of 60'-plus along its western side, and may reach depths over 120' on its seaward side. The reef is noted for its abundance of black sea bass and giant lobster. Native divers call the oversized lobsters "caballos" and "burros" (horses and donkeys), which gives a good indication of their tremendous sizes.

Vessels approaching this reef should exercise extreme caution. Fog may rise quickly in the area, and the reef is exposed to all weather conditions. The reef is littered with ships whose pilots underestimated the dangers. On a windy day with choppy seas, the location of the reef is indistinguishable from the surrounding wave action.

PUNTA SAN CARLOS may be reached by a rough dirt road stretching 45 miles south of El Rosario. A small fishing village lies abreast the large shallow bay called BAHIA SAN CARLOS. There are no tourist facilities in the area, but there are primitive camping sites along the wide expanse of beach, and visitors to the region should be totally self-contained. There is also a small airstrip nearby. Diving excursions may be arranged through the local fishermen in the area, who use small wooden or fiberglass skiffs with 40 h.p. motors. Commercial divers also work in the surrounding waters with hookah compressors.

SAN CARLOS BAY provides a good sheltered anchorage from northwest wind conditions. A small rock island lies immediately off the point, from which it is separated by a large shoal area. A large kelp bed that offers excellent diving lies just southwest of SAN CARLOS POINT, with generally shallow depths ranging from 30' to 60' over rocky bottom. The kelp field is about 2 miles long, and extends out about five miles from shore. There are also some submerged pinnacles in the area which rise to within 20' of the surface.

BLACK SEA BASS
Stereolepis gigas

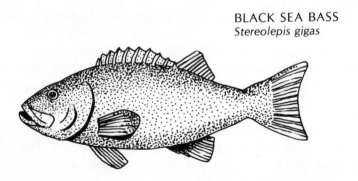

El Rosario to Guerrero Negro

The Pacific ocean coastline southward from Punta San Carlos to Guerrero Negro encompasses approximately 130 miles of open coastline. Baja's Highway 1, which parallels the coast to El Rosario, turns east at El Rosario and curves inland to continue its southward route through the middle of the peninsula, before emerging again near the Pacific Ocean coastline at Guerrero Negro. This section of the coastline is presently largely undeveloped and inaccessible, with only very rough dirt roads leading into coastal areas occupied by small fishing villages. There are no offshore islands along the coast, only a few protected bights for anchoring, and open beaches are generally washed by heavy surf and ocean swells.

One interesting side trip into this section of the coast is the small village of Santa Rosalillita. A wide gravel road turns west from the main highway about 155 miles south of El Rosario for a distance of 10 miles into the tiny settlement of SANTA ROSALILLITA on the Pacific coast. Here a fishing cooperative harvests abalone and other shellfish. There are presently no tourist facilities, but the beaches are excellent for camping and shelling. This area is very popular with surfers, beachcombers and surf fishermen. it is also sometimes possible to arrange diving excursions with the local fishermen.

This section of the highway also gives access to the Northern portion of the Sea of Cortez. The junction leading into Punta Final branches off from the main highway about 123 miles south of El Rosario. A very rough dirt road winds a distance of 47 miles into the Sea of Cortez coast. Future plans for development include the paving of this road into Punta Final, which will then connect with another paved road all the way north to San Felipe via Puertecitos. At the present time, however, the road between Punta Final and Puertecitos is very rough, and recommended for 4-wheel drive only. The junction into the Bay of Los Angeles region is also located along this highway at Parador Punta Prieta, about 140 miles south of El Rosario.

VIZCAINO DESERT

The 220-mile stretch of highway in this section of the peninsula between El Rosario and Guerrero Negro passes through one of North America's most unique desert regions—the Vizcaino Desert. The Vizcaino Desert occupies the west central portion of the Baja peninsula, extending from south of El Roasario to the San Ignacio region. This large desert region is bordered by the Pacific Ocean on its west, which provides a unique source of moisture through the condensation of heavy coastal fogs. Cooling onshore breezes also help prevent extremely high temperatures in the desert during most of the year.

The unique climatic and geological conditions of the Vizcaino Desert have resulted in the development of some very unusual and bizarre plants in Baja California. Some of these include the cardon cacti, the cirio tree, elephant tree, candelilla, and ocotillo.

The cirio tree is one of the most unusual plants in Baja. It is found nowhere else in the world except along the 150-mile stretch of desert between El Rosario and Guerrero Negro. The cirio tree (Idria columnaris) is related to the ocotillo. It is a tall pole-like tree whose tapering trunk branches into clusters of curved and twisted branches at its top. It can grow to heights of 60 feet. it derives its name "cirio" (which is the Spanish word for a long, thick wax-candle) because the plant was thought to resemble the tall wax tapers of the early missions in Baja. It is also occasionally referred to as the "boojum" tree . . . from the name of a mystical desert dwelling creature in Lewis Carroll's story "The Hunting of the Snark."

Chapter 2

Pacific Ocean: Southern Baja

Pacific Ocean: Southern Baja

The Pacific Ocean coastline from Guerrero Negro south to Cabo San Lucas in the state of southern Baja (BAJA CALIFORNIA SUR) is largely undeveloped, with small fishing villages located sporadically along the coast that are accessible by very rough dirt roads, often requiring the use of 4-wheel drive vehicles. There are presently no tourist facilities along this stretch of coastline, and the few diving attractions that are located in this area are accessible only to off-road and self-contained travelers, or to cruisers with long-range boats. One of the main tourist attractions is the whale lagoons, located along the coast from Scammon's Lagoon to Magdalene Bay, where whale-watching activities are popular from January through March each year.

From January through mid-March each year over 6,000 California gray whales travel from the Arctic seas to the protected lagoons along the west coast of Baja California to mate and bear their young. Once hunted nearly to extinction by whalers, today the California gray whale is protected by law and is hunted only by whale-watchers and photographers, who observe the whales from small skiffs as they cavort with their young in the shallow lagoons of Scammon, San Ignacio and Magdalene Bay.

Scammon's Lagoon is named after the man who first discovered the lagoon in the mid-1800's . . . Captain Charles M. Scammon. An enterprising whaler, Scammon returned year after year to the lagoon. Inevitably, the whereabouts of the lagoon was discovered by other whaling ships, and within a few decades the California grays were nearly slaughtered to extinction. Finally, both the United States and Mexican government took steps to protect the grey whale, and

Scammon's Lagoon was officially designated a natural park. The lagoon is a wildlife refuge. It is closed to all unauthorized boats, and diving is permitted in the lagoon without an official permit.

There are a number of locations around the lagoon from which the whales can be observed. One good observation point is the old salt wharf which is located 7 miles west of Guerrero Negro via a rough paved road. A dirt road also leads into the southeast side of the lagoon where the whales can be observed from the national park site. A sign indicating "Parque Natural de Ballena Gris" marks a dirt road that branches off from the main highway about 5 miles south of the Guerrero Negro turnoff. The road is wide and graded, and passable with standard cars. Overnight camping is permitted on the shore of the lagoon, but there are presently no tourist facilities.

Guerrero Negro

The town of Guerrero Negro is not known for its recreational attractions, and holds little of interest for the Baja tourist. It is located about 2 miles west of the main highway just past the site of the large Eagle Monument that marks the boundary between the states of Baja California and Baja California Sur, at the 28th parallel. The town owes its existence to the large salt-producing works that dominates the industry of the town. Guerrero Negro is one of the world's leading producers of salt. The large salt works south of town produces salt through thousands of large evaporating ponds. These ponds are flooded with sea water which then evaporates in the hot desert sun, leaving tons of salt which is harvested and carried to nearby Cedros Island on huge barges. At Cedros Island, the salt is loaded onto large ocean-going freighters and shipped all over the world.

Guerrero Negro does offer adequate facilities and services for travelers, including overnight lodging, a trailer park, cafes, stores, auto parts and mechanics services, gasoline Pemex stations, banks, a hospital, and a domestic airport. Guerrero Negro serves as a good gateway to visit nearby SCAMMON LAGOON for whale watching activities, to explore the remote and wind-swept beaches to the north of town, or to travel along the Vizcaino Peninsula to Malarrimo Beach or Tortugas Bay, where arrangements can be made for diving and fishing trips to Cedros, Natividad or Benitos Islands.

Cedros Island Area

The Cedros Island area includes the offshore islands of San Benitos, Natividad and Cedros. These islands offer exciting diving opportunities, with large fields of kelp, numerous detached pinnacles and submerged reefs close around the shoreline. However, sportdiving around these islands is accessible only to self-contained divers with long-range cruising boats or to off-road travelers chartering local skiffs from fishing villages along the remote and undeveloped Vizcaino peninsula. These islands are very popular with the long-range sportfishing fleet from San Diego. The waters around the islands are known for their abundance of tuna, skipjack, albacore, yellowtail, mackerel, dorado, and black sea bass. The locals also harvest lobster and abalone around the reefs of the islands.

Cedros Island (meaning "Island of Cedars"...so named for the cedar trees found on the island) is the largest island along the west coast of Baja, measuring 21 miles in length. It is located opposite the Baja peninsula at its closest point to land 12 miles N.W. of Punta San Eugenia. Residents of a small village on the south shore of the island are primarily engaged in fishing, harvesting lobster and abalone, operating a cannery, and loading salt off barges from Guerrero Negro onto large ocean-going vessels. There is an airstrip on the island, with domestic flights between Guerrero Negro, Ensenada, Tijuana and La Paz.

Cedros island exhibits an interesting diversity of marine species and habitats. The western shore of the island is fringed with dense fields of kelp close along the shore in depths averaging 60 feet. Marine life on this side of the island is dominated by the cold-water temperate California species. This side is considered the weather side of the islands, as it is exposed to open sea, is frequently washed by heavy surf, is exposed to prevailing northwesterlies, and offers few protected anchorages.

Along the lee shore of the island, which is the eastern side facing towards the Vizcaino Bay, there are protected anchorages all along the coast and water conditions are generally calmer. The lee shore

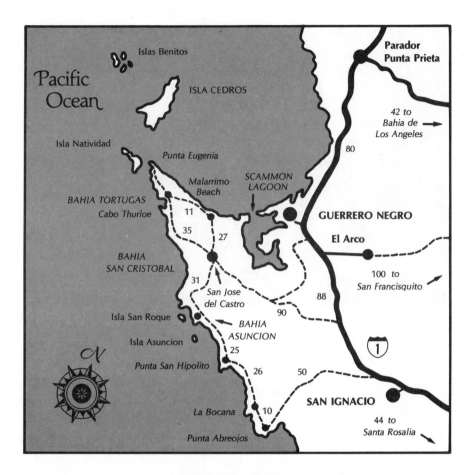

Map labels:
Pacific Ocean
Islas Benitos
ISLA CEDROS
Parador Punta Prieta
42 to Bahia de Los Angeles
80
Isla Natividad
Punta Eugenia
Malarrimo Beach
SCAMMON LAGOON
GUERRERO NEGRO
BAHIA TORTUGAS
Cabo Thurloe
11
35
27
El Arco
BAHIA SAN CRISTOBAL
31
San Jose del Castro
100 to San Francisquito
88
90
Isla San Roque
BAHIA ASUNCION
Isla Asuncion
25
N
Punta San Hipolito
26
50
1
La Bocana
10
SAN IGNACIO
44 to Santa Rosalia
Punta Abreojos

Isla Cedros

faces the large Vizcaino Bay and exhibits the same type of tropical life forms around its reefs as those found in Vizcaino Bay. Vizcaino Bay is considered the northern boundary for several of the tropical Eastern Pacific marine species.

The south shore of the island is bold and rocky, with numerous detached rocks, pinnacles and offshore reefs. Isolated areas of kelp found from 1 to 3 miles off the south shore of the island mark numerous shoal areas that rise out of deep water, with depths generally ranging from 25 to 90 feet over rocky bottom terrain. The islands are often shrouded in mists and heavy fog, and heavy year-round boat traffic in the area, from large freighters and fishing fleets, can be hazards to small boat operators.

Baja's rugged San Benitos Islands are surrounded by rocky pinnacles and kelp beds, but are rarely visited by sportdivers due to their remoteness. (photo: Mia Tegner)

Isla San Benito

San Benito Island is located 20 miles west of Cedros Island. It is comprised of three barren, rocky islands surrounded by detached rocks and kelp. The Benitos islands are considered the most rugged of the island group, and are the least explored. Numerous pinnacle rocks (both submerged and awash), shoal areas, kelp fields, reefs and outlying rocks provided unlimited diving sites around these islands, which are only rarely visited by long range cruising boats. There is a small fishing village on the southeast side of the westernmost Benitos Island. A large sea lion rookery ocupies a cove on Middle Benito Island.

Natividad Island is the island closest to the Baja peninsula, located just 4 miles across the channel from Punta Eugenia. The island is a flat and low-lying island measuring 3 3/4 miles in length, with steep and rocky shores. There is a small fishing village that occupies the southeast end of the island. Several reefs extend off the northwest side of the island, and the island is fringed by kelp beds and large and prominent detached rocks.

Bahia Tortugas Region

The Pacific Ocean coastal region southward of Guerrero Negro all the way to Magdalene Bay is essentially an off-road region, with poor roads and minimal water and gas supplies. The transpeninsular Hiway 1 heads east across the Baja peninsula at Guerrero Negro, then continues south along the Sea of Cortez coastline. Dirt roads branching off from the main highway, however, do lead into numerous small ranches and fish camps along the Pacific Coast, and into miles of interesting bays, coves, lagoons and beaches.

TOURIST FACILITIES

There are no tourist facilities and only limited supplies can sometimes be obtained from the ranches or fishing villages in the region. All camping in the region should be totally self-sufficient. This is a region for the self-contained off-road traveler, preferably with a high-clearance 4-wheel drive vehicle. Many of the roads, however, are well graded and well-marked and are easily passable with standard vehicles, except during the rainy seasons.

FISHING VILLAGES

There are several sizable fishing settlements situated along the coastline from Turtle Bay to Magdalene Bay, as well as numerous smaller fishing camps (some seasonal) along the coast. The usual access into most of the coastal villages is by long-range cruising boat or with small planes.

BAHIA TORTUGAS (Turtle Bay)—is located 340 miles southeast of San Diego, California, and is the best all-weather harbor between San Diego and Magdalene Bay on the Pacific Coast. It is popularly frequented by cruising yachts, where gasoline, water and limited grocery provisions can be obtained. It is located about 100 miles from the main highway over a rough dirt road. A small airport provides domestic air service to Ensenada, Cedros Island and Guerrero Negro. The fishing village supports a small cannery, centered around the local fishing and abalone industries.

BAHIA ASUNCION—lies about 45 miles southward of Turtle Bay. The fishing village of Asuncion is about the same size as Turtle Bay, and also has an airstrip and a cannery. The entire town is supported by the fishing, abalone and lobster industries.

ABREOJOS—The village of Abreojos is situtated about 90 miles south of Asuncion on the coast back of a sheltered anchorage. A dirt road winds along the coast for a distance of 63 miles to connect the two villages. Another dirt road leads from Abreojos to Highway 1, a distance of 53 miles. Both roads are passable with standard cars. An airstrip serves the village, and limited fuel and supplies can be obtained from the locals.

The large lagoon of San Ignacio, located just south of Abreojos, is one of the principal mating and calving lagoons for the California Grey whales. Whale watching activities and scientific observations are conducted in the lagoon between January and mid-March. The usual access to the lagoon is by long-range boat, and most of the large whale watching expeditions originate from San Diego, California.

DIVING

The waters along this section of coastline contain numerous off-lying rocky shoals, some small off-shore islands (notably: San Roque and Asuncion), large kelp beds, large off-shore fishing banks, and submerged reefs and rocks awash extending from prominent points of land. Some of Baja's richest fishing grounds are located in this region. Large Tuna clippers fish the waters for tuna, skipjack, bonita, albacore and yellowtail. Surf fishing and bottom fishing are excellent and abalone, clams and lobster are still abundant. Large kelp beds are located off-shore along the coast.

South of Asuncion near Hipolito Point the large kelp beds disappear, and with the exception of the detached reefs and rocks surrounding Punta Abreojos, the coastline is generally low and sandy. From San Juanico south to Magdalene Bay, a series of lagoons separated from the ocean by sand bars continues for 60 miles along the coast. Thus, best diving possibilities in the region occur between Turtle Bay and Asuncion, as well as in the vicinity of Punta Abreojos. The local abalone divers and lobster fishermen in the small villages are very knowledgeable about the reefs in the surrounding waters, and can be approached for diving guide services and small boat rentals.

Bahia Magdalena

Magdalene Bay (Bahia Magdalena) is situated about 270 miles south of Turtle Bay. The Bay itself is a 17-mile long protected waterway situated opposite the mainland between the long, narrow Isla Santa Margarita on its southern side, and a narrow peninsula of land on its northern shores called Isla Magdalena. It is the largest deep water, all-weather harbor on Baja California's Pacific coastline.

The Mexican navy base of Puerto Cortes is located inside the Bay on Santa Margarita Island. The small village of Puerto San Carlos is located at the north end of the Bay on the mainland side, 30 miles from Cd. Constitution along Baja's Hiway 1 via a good paved road. A deep-water pier at Puerto San Carlos services international commercial boat traffic, and fresh water, gasoline and fresh and canned supplies are available in town.

A SMALL BOAT PARADISE

A series of shallow, inland coastal lagoons which are separated from the sea by narrow strips of sand beach extend another 60 miles north along the coast connecting with Magdalene Bay. These lagoons are navigable by shoal draft small boats, which can be easily launched over the shores. This immense and largely unexplored waterway wilderness system presents unlimited exploration possibilities for the small boater. There are presently no small boat launching ramps along its shores, but future development plans include boat ramps and marinas.

The waters of Magdalene Bay and the surrounding mangrove thickets and salt marshes harbor a myriad of interesting wildlife, including: waterfowl, shellfish, (clams, scallops, oysters), game fish (snook, croaker, corvina), manta ray, sharks, seals and turtles.

DIVING

Commercial local diving activities are carried out around the waters inside the Bay and the surrounding Pacific Ocean waters, primarily for lobster, shellfish and abalone. There are no diving or tourist facilities anywhere in the region, but there are excellent possiblities for self-contained divers. The remains of numerous shipwrecks lie strewn along the coastline from Santa Maria Bay to Cabo Tosco.

Depths are generally shallow, 40′ and less, along the shoreline inside the Bay, which is backed by mangrove thickets or small rock and sand beaches. The best diving areas are generally located along the Pacific Ocean side of Santa Margarita Island, from the middle of the island south to Cabo Tosco. However, the area is usually beset by heavy surge and poor visibility year-round, except during the months from Nov. through Jan., when diving conditions are optimum. Off-shore reefs are characterized by rocky terrain covered with short, thick growths of seaweed, which the locals call "zacate." Cold waters necessitate the use of a 3/16″ to 1/4″ wetsuit.

Whale watching expeditions to Baja's coastal lagoons give man a chance to reach out to a once endangered species....the California Grey Whale.

Todos Santos Region

The Pacific Ocean coastline along Baja California's southern Cape region centers around the small agricultural village of Todos Santos. Todos Santos lies halfway between La Paz and Cabo San Lucas, (see map p. 184: Cape Region). The Todos Santos region is characterized by tropical vegetation (sugar cane, palms, tropical fruit and mango trees), and presents a delightful contrast to the arid desert terrain along the Sea of Cortez shore on the opposite side of the peninsula.

The road from La Paz to Todos Santos (a distance of about 50 miles) is paved, and there is a Pemex station in Todos Santos. The paved road then continues to El Pescadero, a small town just south of Todos Santos. The first layer of an unfinished highway continues from there about 50 miles southward to Cabo San Lucas, but rain and sand have nearly destroyed it, leaving a hard-packed "washboard" surface of earth and sand. This road is passable with standard cars.

A side trip into this coastal region is well worth the inconvenience of a rough road and slow travel. Almost the entire road hugs the coastline, opening onto spectacular panoramic views of the ocean and passing miles of smooth sandy beaches. Several smaller dirt roads turn off from the main road into several nice camping beaches, including San Pedro, Los Esteros and Los Cerritos.

DIVING

There are no sportdiving facilities in the area and tourist facilities are also minimal compared to the developing Cape Region. As far as water recreational activities are concerned in this region, fishing and surfing are number one. Wide, sweeping expanses of sandy beaches afford excellent surf fishing all along the coast, and generally steep shorelines with heavy surf attract surfing enthusiasts. The excellent swimming and camping beaches all along the coast are often less crowded than those along the Sea of Cortez side.

Vast expanses of wind-swept beaches characterize Baja's southern Pacific Ocean coastline.

Sportdiving is not popular along this coast. During most of the year strong ocean swells and heavy surf create poor diving conditions, and there is little protection from prevailing winds along this coastline. However, for the self-contained sportdiver, diving is possible during periods of extreme calm from beach areas where rocky reefs extend from shore or around rocky promontories along the coast. The best months to expect calm seas and good visiblities in this region are generally from November through January.

There are no kelp beds along the coast but there are scatterings of offshore submerged rocky reefs, as well as sunken rocks around prominent points of land. Small car-top or inflatable boats can be launched through the surf along several of the beaches in periods of calm weather. There is a good small boat landing along the beach just north of Punta San Pedro. Diving trips may also be arranged through the local fishermen in their fiberglass skiffs.

One scenic side trip located along this coastline is the ancient lighthouse of Cabo Falso, just 40 minutes west of Cabo San Lucas. Cabo Falso was once thought to be the southernmost tip of Baja. Its almost perfectly preserved lighthouse is perched atop a steep cliff of wind-carved rocks, and towers over miles of breathtaking ocean scenery.

Pacific Ocean Islands

There are three distinct groups of oceanic offshore islands in Mexico's Pacific Ocean waters off the Baja California peninsula. They include: 1. Guadalupe Island 2. Rocas Alijos, and 3. the Revillagigedo Archipelago. These islands range in size from little more than barren rock pinnacles covered with bird guano to large, mountainous desert islands covered with vegetation. They are of primary interest to naturalists, scientists, and sportfishermen. There are no tourist facilities whatsoever on any of the islands, and they are for the most part rugged, remote and isloated. Most of them are uninhabited, except for some small communities of fishermen found on the larger islands.

Baja's oceanic islands are periodically visited by large private and long-range sport boats that originate from either San Diego,California, or from Cabo San Lucas. The greatest attraction of these islands is their excellent fishing grounds. Cruise ships also frequent the northernmost island of Guadalupe to observe the breeding activity of the once-endangered elephant seals that now thrive along its shores. Naturalists are also attracted to these islands to study the endemic species of plant and animal life that have evolved on the islands in a complete state of biological isolation.

Although these islands lie apart from the main stream of diving activities in Baja as a result of their remoteness, they deserve a mention as unspoiled and untouched marine wilderness frontiers that present unlimited exploration opportunities for adventuresome divers. As man constantly pushes and expands the limits of his exploration in the undersea world, the more remote and inaccessible places seem to hold a special allure. Several successful group diving charters have been organized to these remote islands.

Isla Guadalupe

ISLA GUADALUPE (Guadalupe Island) is Mexico's westernmost possession. It lies approximately 220 miles southwest of San Diego, and about 180 miles southwest of Punta Banda. The island is about 20 miles long, and from 2 to 6 miles wide. Guadalupe island is actually the top 1/3 of a great volcanic sea mountain that rises from the ocean floor out of 12,000 feet of water. The island is dotted with volcanic mounds and cinder cones, and it is believed that the island's central volcano may be only dormant, and not extinct.

The coastline of Guadalupe Island reveals bold rocky bluffs, sheer volcanic cliffs, some detached rock pinnacles, and generally deep waters close-to. Depths over 300' appear 1/2 mile offshore. A small village of fishermen occupy a large cove on the southwestern side of the island, and a small number of Naval personnel occupy the Naval Base and Weather Station on the island. In 1922 Guadalupe Island was declared a wildlife refuge. Unauthorized landing has been prohibited since that time, and all wildlife within 3 miles from shore is protected by Mexican law.

Guadalupe Island is noted for the large colonies of elephant seals that breed along its shores. This huge and clumsy marine mammal was once nearly slaughtered to extinction by whalers in the early 1800's. Today, elephant seals are protected by law, and thrive in ever-increasing numbers at Guadalupe Island, which serves as one of the few seal rookery sites left today.

Rocas Alijos

Rocas Alijos (meaning "The Lighters") are a group of barren rock pinnacles that lie off the Pacific Coast of Baja California about 152 miles from the nearest point of land on the peninsula at Punta San Roque. This islocated rock group is comprised of three prominent sheer rocky pinnacles whose steep sides deter any type of landing, and whose largest rock stands just over 100' high. Numerous smaller rocks, both submerged and awash, are also clustered together with them in a group that occupies a small area in the middle of open ocean about 200 yeards in width, and extending about 1/3 mile in a north-south direction.

The alijos Rocks appear to be the vestiges of a once substantial island, which has long since been eroded over the years by the wind and waves, leaving only these sharp rock pinnacles protruding above the water like the masts of some half-sunken ship. To mariners and yachtsmen, these rock pinnacles, which are neither buoyed or marked in any way, present a serious navigational danger to be given as wide a berth as possible. To fishermen, they are a welcome landmark of good fishing grounds, their submarine depths attracting large schools of tuna, skipjack and other game fish.

The large numbers of marine birds, schooling game fish, sharks, whales, sea lions, porpoises, blackfish and other pelagic fish that frequent the area attest to the richness of marine life around the submarine depths of these rocky and barren pinnacles. To sportdivers, the Alijos Rocks stand as promising beacons of adventure, beckoning only the most confident of divers to explore their yet uncharted and unfamiliar depths. Due to their remoteness and their lack of protection from prevailing winds, very few diving expeditions have explored these pinnacles.

Revillagigedos Archipelago

The Revillagigedos Archipelago is the name of an isolated group of islands (Benedicto, Socorro, Partida and Clarion) located several hundred miles south of the Baja California peninsula. The closest island to Cabo San Lucas is BENEDICTO ISLAND, which lies about 220 miles southward. The next and largest island in the chain is SOCORRO ISLAND, which is located 60 miles south of Benedicto. Slightly southwest of Socorro lies ROCA PARTIDA, which is little more than a large group of rocks awash. And, the most distant island is the island of Clarion, located about 370 miles from the tip of Baja.

All of the islands are of volcanic origin. Benedicto Island actually erupted in 1952, forming a prominent volcanic cone about 1,100 feet high that dominates the profile of the island, along with a large lava flow area. All of the islands are uninhabited, except for a small Mexican Naval base and village on the southern tip of Socorro Island. The islands are periodically visited by private, long-range sport boats as well as commercial Tuna Clippers. Fishing grounds around the Archipelago are excellent, and are noted for large schools of Wahoo and giant yellowfin tuna. Socorro Island is considered to be one of the most spectacular bottom and game fishing areas north of the Galapagos Islands.

The Baja Explorador charter dive boat anchored at the volcanic, Benedicto Island during an expedition to this remote archipelago.

The Revillagigedos Archipelago are a virtually pristine marine wilderness, undisturbed by man's intrusion over countless centuries. Vast numbers of marine birds nest around the islands; giant sea turtles lay their eggs on sandy beaches; California grey whales give birth to their young in warm lagoons around the islands; sea lions inhabit the rocky shores and ledges; a myriad of colorful reef fish inhabit the shallows; and large schools of jacks, tuna, sharks, dolphins, and rays school in the surrounding sea.

One severe limiting factor for visiting this distant island group is its weather patterns. The summer hurricane season is a full 5 months long, with the possibility of hurricane activity occuring from June through October, and occasionally in May and November as well. Nearly every hurricane that the Pacific Ocean generates collides with the Archipelago. September marks the peak of hurricane season, with an average of two or three hurricanes. During the winter months, from November through March, the oceanic weather conditions exhibit strong winds and heavy waves. Thus, the only months to expect stable weather conditions in the area would be late fall, November or early December, and late spring, April or May.

Chapter 3
The Sea of Cortez:
An Overview

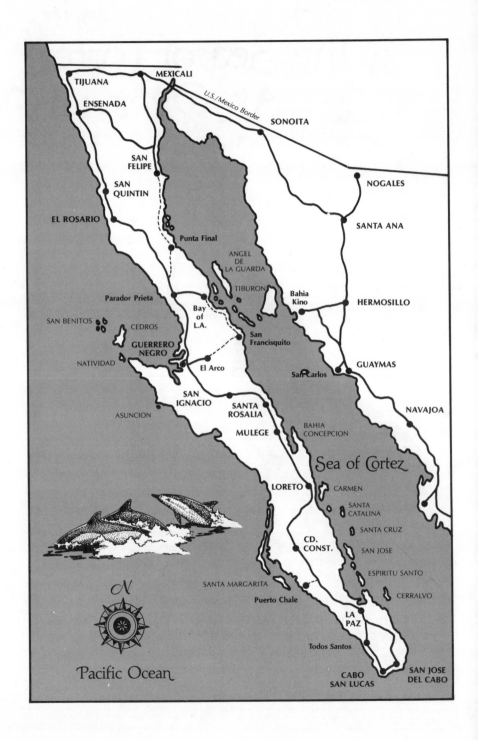

TIJUANA

ENSENADA

MEXICALI

U.S./Mexico Border

SONOITA

NOGALES

SAN FELIPE

SAN QUINTIN

SANTA ANA

EL ROSARIO

Punta Final

ANGEL DE LA GUARDA

TIBURON

Bahia Kino

HERMOSILLO

Parador Prieta

Bay of L.A.

San Francisquito

SAN BENITOS

CEDROS

GUERRERO NEGRO

NATIVIDAD

El Arco

San Carlos

GUAYMAS

SAN IGNACIO

SANTA ROSALIA

NAVAJOA

ASUNCION

MULEGE

BAHIA CONCEPCION

Sea of Cortez

LORETO

CARMEN

SANTA CATALINA

SANTA CRUZ

CD. CONST.

SAN JOSE

ESPIRITU SANTO

SANTA MARGARITA

CERRALVO

Puerto Chale

LA PAZ

N

Todos Santos

CABO SAN LUCAS

SAN JOSE DEL CABO

Pacific Ocean

The Sea of Cortez

The Sea of Cortez is Baja California's foremost water recreational attraction. It is a long and narrow body of water that begins at the Colorado River Delta and ends by converging with the Pacific Ocean at the tip of the Baja peninsula. Its waters are graced with over 100 islands and pinnacles, and its shores are fringed by miles of pristine, sandy beaches, secluded coves, and rocky headlands. The natural mountain and desert barriers of the Baja peninsula have largely hindered the advance of industrial forces along its shores. The Sea of Cortez is still a vast and primitive marine wilderness area, little changed since native Indians first sailed their hand-carved canoes across its jeweled surface.

The Sea of Cortez is one of the youngest of all the seas upon the earth's surface. Its formation occurred through a geological upheaval that began over 25 million years ago, when the Baja peninsula was still a part of mainland Mexico. A gradual shifting of plates in the earth's crust caused the Baja peninsula to split away from the west coast of Mexico, creating a deep chasm that filled with water to create the Sea of Cortez. A scattered chain of offshore islands emerged later through gravitational slidings and volcanic eruptions. Some of these islands are actual remnants of dead volcanoes, but most of them are the tops of half-submerged mountains that slowly split apart from the new peninsula and slid off into the newly-formed sea.

EL MAR DE CORTEZ

The Sea of Cortez derives its name in honor of Hernando Cortez, the early conqueror of Mexico who defeated the great Aztec ruler Montezuma in 1520. Following rumors of fabulous Aztec treasures in the unexplored islands to the west of Mexico (known as Isle of Santa Cruz), Cortez outfitted several expeditions to explore the region, and landed near La Paz in 1535. He failed to find the fabled Aztec treasure, but he found a great abundance of valuable pearl oysters in the waters of the region, which stimulated further expeditions and colonization attempts. One of the later expeditions led by Francisco de Ulloa sailed all the way north to the mouth of the Colorado River, discovering to their surprise that the "Isle of Santa Cruz" was really a peninsula, and not an island after all. Ulloa named the sea he had charted and explored "El Mar de Cortez," after his great leader and benefactor, Hernando Cortez. And the peninsula soon thereafter became known as Lower California, or Baja California.

The Sea of Cortez was also referred to by later European explorers as the "Mar Vermejo," which means the "Vermilion Sea" . . . so named due to the vermilion-colored plankton that periodically blankets its surface. It was also designated as "El Golfo de California," and is labeled today on most U.S. maps as the "Gulf of California." This name is used interchangeably with the Sea of Cortez, and it is very often simply referred to as the "Gulf."

ISLANDS IN TIME

Over 100 primeval looking islands and islets lie scattered along almost the entire length of the Sea of Cortez. These islands are true desert islands. Very few of them have fresh water sources, and most of the islands have a dry and barren appearance, their rocky escarpments dotted only with occasional scrub brush and cactus or covered with bird guano. The islands are nearly all uninhabited, except for some salt and gypsum mining activity and seasonal fish camps. Scorpions, snakes, mice, lizards, rodents, bats and birds comprise their main inhabitants, although some of the islands (Tiburon, Cerralvo, and San Jose) house larger animals such as mule deer, coyotes, iguanas and wild goats.

BROWN PELICAN
Pelecanus occidentalis

These islands occupy a very important place in our ecosystem. Hundreds of species of wildlife that have been pushed out of their natural habitats elsewhere because of population pressures or environmental pollution find sanctuary and haven in Baja's remote islands. The brown pelican, once an endangered species whose nesting areas along the Pacific Ocean were nearly wiped out by the deadly effects of DDT, now thrives in ever-increasing numbers throughout the rocky islands of the Gulf. The Heermans gulls and two species of terns (Elegant and Royal Terns) migrates in vast numbers every year to Raza Island in the Northern Gulf. These birds come from as far away as South America to nest and produce their young on this tiny island in the Sea of Cortez.

Through centuries of isolation, strange and unusual life forms have evolved on several of the islands. Catalan Island boasts the only species of rattleless rattlesnake in the world, and also supports the largest barrel cactus (BIZNAGA) found in Baja. The tiny island of San Esteban houses a lizard called a chuckawalla that is unique. There are other chuckawallas in the world, but the San Esteban chuckawalla is a foot longer, ten times heavier, and more brilliantly colored than its mainland relatives. A very rare species of black jack rabbit resides on Espiritu Santo Island, and there are many other endemic species on the islands that have changed their form slightly, exhibiting the Galapagos-like evolutionary pattern of adaptation to their isolated environments.

The great numbers of sea birds around Baja's offshore islands attest to the richness of marine life in the Sea of Cortez. (photo: Tim Means)

Marine life also flourishes in rich profusion around Baja's desert islands, providing some of the most rewarding sportdiving that the Sea of Cortez has to offer. Rising out of the depths in stark contrast to their surrounding crystalline waters, these off-shore islands are a spectacular sight. Their isolated beaches strewn with driftwood and shells are paradisiacal, yet primitive; their barren, desert terrain belies the fertile richness of their waters; and their sheer granite walls and grotesque rock formations create an awesome type of rugged beauty that sets these "islands in time" apart from any place else in the world.

TIDES AND CURRENTS

The Sea of Cortez has very little wave action of its own, owing to its narrow width, and to its protection from the Pacific Ocean swells. Wave action in the Sea of Cortez is caused only by local winds or extreme tidal activity, and most of the time its tranquil surface appears as a large, glassy inland lake. Violent local storms (known as "chubascos") and tropical hurricanes occasionally appear during the months of August and September. These storms often seem to appear suddenly out of nowhere, bringing with them heavy seas and winds of devastating strength.

The Sea of Cortez is one of the world's largest really deep gulfs, with a depth over 11,000 feet at its lower end. Although the Sea of Cortez has little or no lunar tide of its own, it reacts to the Pacific Ocean lunar tides, which generate extreme tidal fluctuations and swift tidal currents in the narrow, upper region of the Sea of Cortez. Stimulated by the rise in water level caused by Pacific Ocean tides, the Sea of Cortez responds by acting like a giant front of rising water moving up the Gulf.

In the central and lower Gulf, tidal fluctuations of minimal impact are produced. However, when this rising surge of water is abruptly squeezed through the deep basins of the narrow midriff region, strong currents of up to ten or more knots are produced as the water is forced through its narrow submarine canyons. When this great surge of water finally reaches the Colorado River at the northern end, it can produce tides as high as 30 feet on a maximum spring rise, exerting enough pressure to create a tidal bore that causes the river to flow backwards.

Sportdivers in the Northern Sea of Cortez region should be aware of how the tides and currents correspond to the lunar cycle in order to plan diving activities. The tidal currents and fluctuations in the Sea of Cortez reach their peaks at each new and full moon, exhibiting their maximum strength and rise. These tidal currents in the Northern Gulf region can create hazardous diving conditions.

THE CORTEZ FOOD CHAIN

Life begets life a million times over in the Sea of Cortez, attesting to the unique combinaton of elements that fuels nature's dynamic food

73

chain. Chemical conditions in the Sea of Cortez are ideal for producing rich growths of plankton, the basic food supply directly or indirectly for all marine-dwelling animals. The greatest periods of plankton production, or plankton "blooms," in the Sea of Cortez occurs during February and March, when vermilion-colored plankton (FLAGELLATE INFUSORIA) blanket the water in vast numbers, causing the water to appear colored and cloudy. Other types of plankton, especially such minute crustaceans as the opossum shrimp, also become so thickly concentrated at times that swimming through these tiny creatures is like being caught in an underwater snowstorm.

Cold-water upwellings in the Sea of Cortez are also vital to sustaining the food chain and supporting plankton growth. The ocean floor of the Gulf is made up of underwater mountains, canyons and irregular terrain interspersed with broad, continuous areas of regular rock and sand bottoms. Cold-water upwellings are produced when the cold, deep-water currents flowing through the Gulf are forced upward to the surface as they collide with the steep underwater mountains and canyon walls that obstruct their normally smooth flow. These cold-water upwellings bring great quantities of nutrients up from the depths to mix with the oxygen-rich surface waters. The constant circulation of these nutrients is vital to the survival of the rich profusion of marine flora and fauna that flourishes around the submarine reefs in the Sea of Cortez.

The great abundance of marine mammals in the Sea of Cortez also attests to a bountiful food chain. Large colonies of sea lions make their homes around rocky ledges throughout the Sea of Cortez, thriving on a seemingly endless supply of food from the depths. Several types of dolphins and porpoises reside in or visit the Cortez, and many types of whales either reside in or make annual migrations to the Sea of Cortez. Killer whales, false killer whales, blue whales, humpback whales, sperm whales, pilot whales, and the giant plankton-eating finback whales are all attracted to the rich supply of foodstuff in the Sea of Cortez.

Finally, the great population of marine birds in the Sea of Cortez provide the airborn link in the dynamic food chain. Vast numbers of fish-eating birds that thrive in the Sea of Cortez contribute to balancing the oceanic food chain in a very important way. Most marine birds tend to feed on the weaker and diseased members of the fish community, which are naturally slower and easier to pluck up from the depths. This helps keep the fish populations healthy and free of

The osprey is one of the most magnificent of the marine birds that nest along the Sea of Cortez coastline.

diseases, thus contributing to natural selective breeding. The most abundant of the birds in the Cortez are the pelicans, frigate birds, boobies, terns and gulls; the most magnificent is the osprey, who often nests on top of rocky summits or in giant cactus tops; and of exquisite beauty are the egrets, herons and other rare species of shore birds found along the shoreline of the Sea of Cortez.

THE GIANT FISH TRAP

The Sea of Cortez is considered to be one of the most fertile bodies of water in the world. It exhibits a very wide diversity of aquatic habitats, including rocky shores, sandy beaches, rocky reef patches, islands, submerged pinnacles, and mud and tidal flats. This great diversity of habitats supports a rich fish fauna of over 800 species, including pelagic and deep-sea fishes. Many fish species migrate annually into and out of the Cortez, but most have taken up permanent residence in the nutrient-rich waters, and do their migrating entirely within the Cortez. The Sea of Cortez is home to a wondrous variety of marine fishes, from cold-water California-related species to tropical and semi-tropical Caribbean and Panamic species.

Scientific studies of the zoogeographical characteristics of shore fish in the Sea of Cortez have shown that the greatest percentage of the species are related to the Panamic fauna (tropical). The Panamic or tropical fauna in the Sea of Cortez represents those species originating in Central and South America. For millions of years, migrating marine species have traveled northward along the Pacific Coast of Mexico and have been funneled into the narrow reaches of the Sea of Cortez, where an abundant food supply and favorable water temperatures and habitats have caused them to remain and reproduce. It is easy to imagine the Sea of Cortez as a giant funnel constantly trapping fish from Central and South America to fill its vast depths.

Some of the tropical fauna in the Gulf have their origins in the Caribbean. These species were able to immigrate from the Caribbean millions of years ago via a now extinct water connection between the Atlantic and Pacific Oceans, theorized to have been where Panama is today. Over millions of years, these original Caribbean species evolved into distinct, but similar subspecies or new species. Most of the sponges and hydroids in the Sea of Cortez originated in the Caribbean, and many types of morays, sea basses, snappers and grunts bear striking similarities to Caribbean species.

The Sea of Cortez also has many fish in common with the California (temperate) fauna. Many occur only in the colder regions of the Northern Gulf, and may have migrated through the Southern Gulf during periods when water temperatures were low enough to permit their survival enroute. The California red lobster (PANULIRUS) flourishes in the Northern Gulf, and can also be found in the deeper, cold waters of the Central Gulf. There are also a large number of endemic species in the Sea of Cortez, as well as a number of insular species (notably in the Cape region) shared with the off-shore islands of Socorro, Clarion and the Galapagos. The southern Cape region near Cabo San Lucas existed as an island millions of years ago, attracting its own insular species of fish which have remained in the area to the present day.

DIVING THE SEA OF CORTEZ

The Sea of Cortez is an exciting diving destination. It would be difficult to describe diving conditions in the Sea of Cortez in a nutshell; suffice it to say that the water conditions and seasons vary so radically from north to south that it is often difficult to believe that it's all the same sea. It has an unusually wide fluctuation of water temperatures, with temperatures ranging from 50 to 90 degrees F. Waters in the northern Gulf are usually so cold that a ¼" wetsuit is necessary year-round; while the semi-tropical waters of the southern region can reach upwards of 90 degrees F. Water visibilities can also vary greatly, from under ten feet to over 100 feet. Visibilities are disturbed by seasonal plankton growths, by local wind conditions, tidal currents and, of course, hurricane activity. At its worst, diving in the Sea of Cortez can be like diving in pea soup; at its best, like diving in tropical Caribbean waters.

Water temperatures in the Sea of Cortez do not support the growth of hard coral reefs. However, one notable exception to this is the Cabo Pulmo area in the Cape region, where the only living hard coral reef in the Sea of Cortez is located along the bottom of a warm and shallow bay. Generally, the reefs in the Sea of Cortez are comprised of large boulders and rocks and granite pinnacles, often lined with gorgonian corals and sea fans, sporadic patches of hard corals, and various types of sponge and other invertebrate life. The gorgonian corals and sea fans in the Sea of Cortez appear in a

The submarine environment of the Sea of Cortez is comprised of rocky reefs that are often lined with colorful sea fans, and that house a fascinating variety of marine life....such as this unusual striped zebra moray eel.

magnificent variety of sizes and shapes, and generally contribute most of the color to the otherwise barren-looking rock reefs. In the Northern Gulf, sponges are much larger and more dominant along the reefs than in the Central or Southern Gulf.

While beach diving is possible from many areas of the shoreline, with lots of opportunities for good shelling and snorkeling, diving from the beach is generally limited by the lack of access roads to the coast. Inshore diving is most productive along the rocky promotories and headlands extending seaward into the Gulf. Generally the most picturesque and profuse concentrations of marine life that the Sea of Cortez has to offer will be found around the rugged chain of off-shore islands or near off-shore submerged reefs and pinnacles. A notable exception is the southernmost Cape region. In the Cabo San Lucas area, there are several excellent diving locations within a short distance from the beach, and within walking distance of beach-front hotels.

One of the foremost diving attractions of the Sea of Cortez is its overwhelming abundance of marine life, including both resident reef species and pelagics. This adds a unique element of adventure to diving the Sea of Cortez, in that divers often never know what they may encounter next. Divers in the Sea of Cortez have had occasion to swim with such magnificent creatures as black marlin, giant whale sharks, large manta rays, playful sea lions, schools of hammerhead sharks, and other large pelagic fish including roosterfish, barracuda, yellowtail, jacks, and dorado. In between diving destinations in the Sea of Cortez, divers also enjoy the company of sleek whales and playful dolphins performing graceful acrobatics on the mirrored surface of the water. Anchored at night in a secluded cove silhouetted by a fiery sunset, most divers inevitably come to the realization that scuba diving is just a small part of the total charm and beauty of this unique marine wilderness.

Chapter 4
Northern
Sea of Cortez

Northern Sea of Cortez

The northern region of Baja's Sea of Cortez, extending from the mouth of the Colorado River south to Santa Rosalia, has traditionally been a mecca for boaters and sportfishermen. Small towns along the coast offer ample facilities for boating activities including fuel, launching sites, trailer parks and fishing resorts with small landing strips. Numerous islands, along the coast have good small boat anchorages and there is a great abundance of game fish in the surrounding waters.

There is a notable lack of diving facilities in the Northern gulf region, and only one resort (located at San Francisquito Bay) caters to sportdivers. At the present time, there are no dive shops anywhere along the coast, few reliable air compressors for tank fills, and there are no charter dive boats operating regular tours. The greatest reasons for the lack of diving facilities in this region are the harsh tidal conditions combined with seasonal wind activity. Tidal activity in this region of the Gulf produces some of the greatest tides and swiftest currents in the entire Sea of Cortez, presenting distinct drawbacks to sportdiving.

Aside from the harsh tidal conditions, however, off-shore reefs team with marine life, and submerged rocks, pinnacles, and off-shore islands offer good diving locations that are still relatively unexplored. For the self-contained and experienced divers, this region is an untouched frontier of diving opportunities.

NORTHERN GULF MARINE ENVIRONMENT

The Northern Gulf is characterized by a harsh and physically unstable submarine environment. The water exhibits a tremendous annual fluctuation in sea-surface temperatures, ranging from about 55° to 90° F. Tidal activity in the Northern Gulf produces some of the largest tides in the world, with vertical displacement as high as 20 to 30 feet, and currents as strong as ten knots. Cold-water upwellings, especially around the midriff islands (near the Bay of Los Angeles), also produce strong water disturbances.

There are fewer reef fish in the Northern Gulf in comparison to other parts of the Gulf, and the submarine environment is generally considered more temperate than tropical. Reef fish in the Northern Gulf must belong to cold-tolerant species that are able to sur-vive the low sea temperatures in the wintertime. These colder winter temperatures periodically cause "winterkills" of several species, most notably the Panamic sergeant major, which often suffers great seasonal declines in its population, but appears to re-bound successfully.

Some of the more dominant cold-tolerant species in this region include the Gulf opaleye, Panamic sergeant major, clinids, gobys, spotted sand bass, rock wrasse, and sargo. Triggerfish, pufferfish, Cortez angelfish, grunts, cabrilla, snappers, grouper and spiny lobster also inhabit the reefs. The waters are cold enough to suit several California species, including the red lobster. (PANULIRUS), sheepshead, and lingcod. Common pelagic game fish in the region include: yellowtail, sea bass, mackerel, roosterfish, jacks, corvina, and totuava (now protected by law).

As is typical throughout the Sea of Cortez, submarine reefs are formed by submerged rocks and boulders. The off-shore islands are the peaks of large marine mountains that project from great depths, and some of the islands are actual volcanoes. Their submarine reefs and ledges vary dramatically in appearance from barren rock surfaces to colorful areas covered with lush growths of sponges, soft corals and diverse invertebrate life. Sporadic growths of kelp are also common throughout the region. Cold waters prohibit the growth of hard corals, but soft gorgonian corals and sea fans grow profusely. Sponge life is more prolific along reefs in this region than elsewhere in the Sea of Cortez.

The Common Dolphin (Delphinus delphis), which can reach up to 7 feet in length, is often seen in large schools in the Sea of Cortez.

The large plankton-eating finback whale, which can reach up to 80 feet in length, is a permanent resident of the Northern Gulf midriff region. The second largest of all animals on earth, these mighty creatures may be seen in pods of as many as 20 or more whales traveling together. The green sea turtle was once plentiful in the region, but recent over-harvesting has greatly depleted its numbers. Sea lion rookeries abound, and porpoises, dolphins, orcas, and rays grace the waters. A seemingly endless variety of bird life also attests to the richness of sea life in the Northern Sea of Cortez.

WEATHER AND WATER CONDITIONS

The Northern Sea of Cortez Region enjoys pleasant weather during the winter and spring months, with prevailing winds appearing in periods of two to three days' duration, then subsiding for a short period to produce several days of calm weather. The summer and early fall months produce hot weather, with extreme periods of heat during the summer.

NOVEMBER THRU MAY: During these months, gale force northwesterly winds may arise intermittently, but they are generally of short duration, followed by periods of calm. The strength and duration of these winds greatly influences sportdiving conditions. On windy days visibility may average less than 30 feet, and short, choppy surface waves produce uncomfortable conditions for small boat maneuvering, water entries, and surface swimming. However, periods of prolonged calm during this season can produce water visibilities of 50' and more, with excellent sportdiving conditions. Plankton blooms occur sporadically in February and March, which greatly disturbs water visibility.

In the spring months, a mild wind generally arises in the afternoon and cools the hot daytime temperatures, which can reach over 100° F. when breezes fail. April and May provide the most comfortable daytime weather, with more periods of prolonged calm, when diving is at its best.

JUNE THRU OCTOBER: Hot and gusty winds from the desert frequently disturb the otherwise hot and still weather in the summertime. Southeasterly winds also prevail, with uncomfortable daytime temperatures when winds subside. Plankton blooms may also occur in June and July, and miniscule fish larvae and small fry frequently congregate in shallower depths, greatly reducing water visibility. The later fall months experience somewhat milder weather and frequent periods of calm. During these months, diving activities are best during the morning hours, as prevailing winds tend to arise in the afternoon.

FINBACK WHALE
Balaenoptera physalus

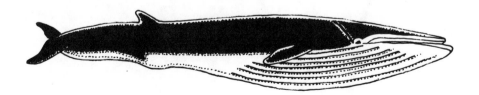

31 to Jct.
Hiway 3 & 5

SAN FELIPE

Punta Radar

Playa Hermosa

Campo Perlita

48

Playa Mexico

El Coloradito

Sea of Cortez

Puertecitos

El Herfanito

76 to El Rosario

Isla Miramar

54

Isla Lobos

Isla Encantada

①

Isla San Luis

Punta Bufeo

Catavina

Punta Willard

Isla Willard

BAHIA SAN LUIS GONZAGA

64

Punta Final

38

Nueva Chapala

84

San Felipe Region

The coastline between San Felipe and the Bay of Los Angeles, comprising the uppermost portion of the Sea of Cortez, is generally low and sandy, with gently sloping shorelines. This region of the Sea of Cortez caters almost exclusively to sportfishermen, with sportfishing resorts dotting the coastline from San Felipe south. Most of the sportfishing resorts in the region have good launching ramps for trailered boats, good supplies of aviation and marine fuel, small airstrips, and trailer campsites.

The major tourist centers are SAN FELIPE, easily reached by a good paved hiway from Mexicali, and PUERTECITOS, a popular sportfishing center 45 miles south of San Felipe that is accessible by a well-traveled dirt road. Both of these towns are dominated by commercial and tourist fishing enterprises, and have ample facilities for visitors, including gas, ice, butane, restaurants, resort accommodations, trailer sites, beach camping and grocery provisions.

Sportdiving in this area is limited by the great tidal fluctuations, a generally sandy coastline with relatively shallow depths offshore, and the total lack of diving facilities. Water visibilities are almost continuously disturbed by turbidity from rivers, by tidal currents and plankton blooms. The great tidal range (with vertical displacement as high as 20 to 30 feet) causes very strong currents, creating severe sea conditions particularly when the wind and currents oppose each other. However, when conditions are good, sportdiving is enjoyable for the self-contained diver around rocky points and reefs sporadically found along the coast, as well as around the chain of offshore islands called the ENCANTADOS.

THE ISLAS ENCANTADOS (ENCHANTED ISLANDS) are the northernmost group of Gulf islands. They are comprised of a six-island archipelago that lies close offshore in a chain between Punta Bufeo and Punta Fermin, stretching for 20 miles opposite an unbroken beach beginning 29 miles south of PUERTECITOS. They include the islands of:

A diver stops to examine the round stingray, a common bottom dweller in the Sea of Cortez.

SAN LUIS, LA POMO, LOS LOBOS, MIRAMAR, ENCANTADA, and EL HUERFANITO. These islands are characterized by harsh volcanic features, with red and black lava rock dominating their surfaces, and by the great flocks of seabirds that congregate near their shores.

One of the small islands, ISLA LA POMO, is actually one large chunk of pumice stone that has the peculiar characteristic of being lighter by volume than water. Large chunks of pumice stone often crack off from its steep sides, and float around neighboring islands as they are carried away by currents. These strange floating rocks, weird volcanic formations, and strong currents caused the natives and early explorers to name this group of islands the "enchanted or bewitched" islands.

Depths offshore from these islands are generally shallow, but some detached rocks (awash at low tide) and submerged reefs around the islands offer good sportdiving sites when water conditions are good. Grouper and Gulf opaleye are common, along with typical Northern Gulf marine life.

Bay of Los Angeles Region

The Bay of Los Angeles region (BAHIA DE LOS ANGELES) boasts a unique array of offshore islands, a fine sheltered harbor, numerous sheltered coves and beaches, and a small settlement slowly expanding to meet increasing tourist demands. A trip by car from the border at Tijuana covers a distance of about 415 miles, all over paved roads with reliable gasoline stops and miles of interesting desert scenery. The turn-off from the main highway is well marked and is located at Parador Punta Prieta.

The Bay of Los Angeles is one of the few areas in the Northern Gulf that affords accessible diving locations from shore by small boats. It has been a popular sportdiving destination for many years, even though it has seldom offered diving facilities for tourists. Today, it is a popular sportdiving destination for groups who bring their own compressors and who dive from small boats, totally self-contained. Tidal conditions are not quite as extreme as those to the north, and deep-water upwellings tend to keep water visibilities clearer. With over a dozen offshore islands just off its coast, the Bay of Los Angeles affords ample sportdiving sites.

TOURIST FACILITIES

Tourist facilities in the Bay of Los Angeles area are located on the main street of the small town by the same name. Presently, there are two resort hotels which are prominently visible and are located within walking distance of each other. Each has their own charter boats, and can arrange sportfishing or diving trips. There are several small restaurants in town, (as well as in the hotel dining rooms), and several markets offer a limited supply of fresh and canned goods, as well as beer and liquor. Block and cubed ice is available from an ice house in town, providing the generator is functioning.

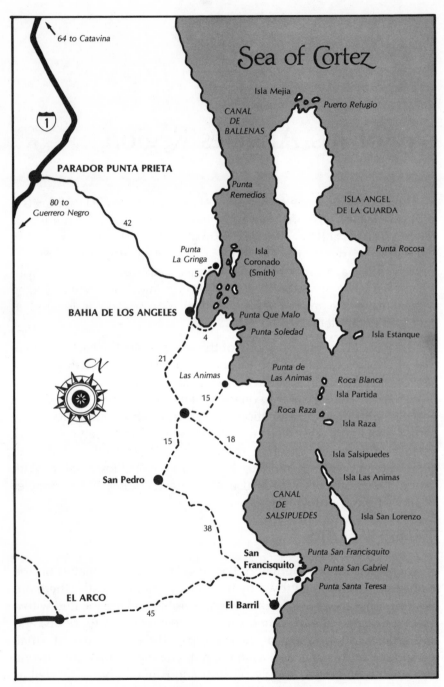

Bay of Los Angeles Region

A trailer and RV park is located on the waterfront next to the PEMEX gas station, with water and electrical hook-ups. Water in the Bay of Los Angeles is obtained from an underground well, and is very safe to drink. Public beach camping is allowed on the sand dunes north and south of town, but there are no facilities.

A small plane landing strip is presently located in the center of the town, but a larger airstrip is now under construction just north of town. With its completion, the Bay of Los Angeles may sustain greater contact with the outside world. At present, there are no telephone communications into the region, and all communication is done by radio. Postal service and bus services are periodic, and there are no hospital or medical facilities in town. In case of medical emergencies, small planes from the landing strip are usually summoned to evacuate patients or to bring in supplies.

BOAT LAUNCHING

A good paved boat launching ramp is located next to the PEMEX gasoline station facing the harbor. For a small fee, boats of all sizes can be launched into the bay. Small car-top boats and smaller trailered boats may be launched over the beach both north and south of the bay along the coast, but KEEP AN EYE OUT FOR TIDE CHANGES.

Larger charter boats can be rented from either of the two hotels in town. Smaller launches and fiberglass skiffs (called "PANGAS") are available from local fishermen, or where local signs indicate.

DIVING THE BAY OF LOS ANGELES

There are presently no diving facilities or reliable air fill stations at the Bay of Los Angeles. However, sometimes airfills can be obtained from a small compressor located at the curio store next to the PEMEX station, but this service is not always reliable. Boats with dive guides can also sometimes be chartered through the same store. It is presently best to bring extra tanks or your own compressor to dive the Bay of Los Angeles.

Because of poor coastal access, a minimum of beach diving is available around this region. Most of the diving locations along the coast are accessible by boat only. The Bay of Los Angeles is an ideal place to bring your own boat, from small inflatables to wooden skiffs or larger yachts. A good variety of sportdiving is easily accessible from small boats.

WETSUITS—Because of the year-round cool water temperatures, a wetsuit of 3/16 to 1/4-inch thickness is recommended for warmth during normal periods of immersion with scuba equipment. Water temperatures are much cooler in this region of the Sea of Cortez than either to the north or south. Cold currents from the deep submarine trenches are constantly being forced to the surface by the tidal activity in the region. Water temperatures, even in the warmer months, rarely exceed 75° F.

TIDES—Tides in the Bay of Los Angeles region average 8 feet, and exhibit a maximum spring rise of 12 feet. The considerable range in tidal movement, plus the narrow width and numerous islands located in this region, combine to create strong tidal currents, particularly around the group of islands in the narrow midriff region. These tidal currents can present hazards to sportdiving, particularly when coupled with adverse wind conditions.

A reliable compass is a must for diving in the Bay of Los Angeles region. Should tidal currents or winds arise rapidly, a scuba diver should be prepared to maneuver against adverse conditions underwater with the use of a good compass.

Both the wind conditions and lunar periods should be taken into account as an important part of pre-dive planning in this region. Know what the tidal activity is doing, and plan to dive during periods of slack tide or during periods of minimal lunar influence. REMEMBER: Tidal currents are at their maximum strength on each full and new moon, and DIMINISH in force during half-moon periods. By studying the tides, we've often found it easy to take advantage of medium-strength tidal currents to enjoy "drift-diving" along with the current, with a reliable person at the helm of a boat to follow our movements.

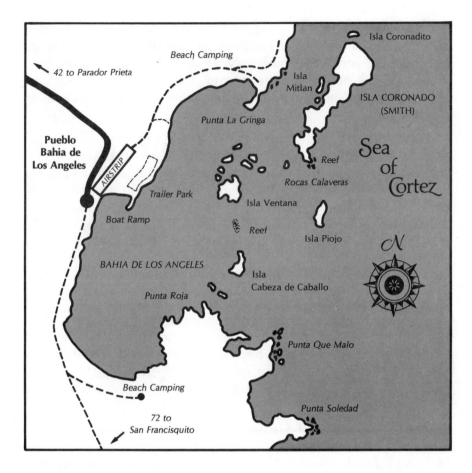

DIVING LOCATIONS

Bahia de Los Angeles

The coastal and offshore region surrounding the town of the Bay of Los Angeles includes numerous islands and reefs which are easily reached by boat from any point around the bay. This area contains a number of excellent diving locations, many just a short distance from camping sites and trailer park facilities. (NOTE: all depths indicated in diving locations are depths taken at mean tide intervals.)

PUNTA LA GRINGA is located at the northwestern end of the bay. Good sportdiving sites are located about 1 1/2 miles north of the point, just opposite ISLA MITLAN. Several large groupings of detached rocks along the coast form good-sized underwater reefs located about

150' offshore. The reefs are hidden from view at extreme high tides, but they appear with water awash as the tide recedes. Depths range between 20' and 50' immediately around the larger rocks, then gradually slope deeper into the channel. The reefs are noted for their abundance of brightly colored sponges, as well as a good population of game fish.

ISLA MITLAN lies midway along the western shores of CORONADO ISLAND (also called SMITH ISLAND), to which it is connected by a low-lying rocky shoal area. A scenic sheltered bay lies between the two islands, with an excellent landing beach for small boats, and good snorkeling in the shallows. The best scuba site lies at the northern tip of the islet, where the rocky shoreline drops to depths of 40', then gradually slopes to deeper waters over a rocky bottom. Underwater terrain around the islet reveals almost no invertebrate life, but reef fish and some schooling fish appear among the rocks.

ISLA CORONADO (also SMITH ISLAND) is the largest of the islands in the immediate bay vicinity. It measures 4 miles in length, with a volcano-like peak at its northern end. Good landing beaches are located toward the middle of both sides of the island. Generally, the western side of the island is not well suited for sportdiving because of barren rock and cobblestone bottoms that slope abruptly into the main channel.

The eastern side of the island exhibits diverse underwater terrain, ranging from barren rock piles to colorful reefs teeming with marine life. Good diving reefs are located just offshore, from the middle of the island to its southern tip, where detached rocks (awash at low tide) indicate the locations of submerged reefs. Depths around these reefs range from 20' and less to over 80', as rock and sand bottoms drop rapidly seaward. Gulf opaleye, sheephead and spotted sand bass are common around these reefs, as are several varieties of colorful nudibranchs.

Immediately off the SOUTHEASTERN TIP of CORONADO ISLAND a large ridge of rocks continues underwater in a southeasterly direction, several hundred yards seaward. This reef is partially visible at low tide, and is an outstanding diving location. Depths range from 20' near shore to more then 80' on the outer edges of the reef. Both close-up and wide angle photography are productive, with a variety of fish and invertebrate life around the reef.

Looking over the inner Bay of Los Angeles islands, with Smith Island in the background. (photo: Lyn Freeman)

ISLA CORONADITO is the small islet at the northern tip of CORONADO ISLAND, separated from the larger island by a deep, narrow channel on its south shore. The channel is noted for its heavy currents and an abundance of big-game fish. The south side of the islet, facing the channel has a rocky shoreline with sharp drop-offs, providing excellent diving terrain. The northern and western sides of the islet are better suited for snorkeling and shallow diving, with depths of 40′ and less within 100 yards from shore. Protected coves for small boat anchorages may be found in the lee of the island. The rocky underwater terrain is lacking in invertebrate life, but crevices and ledges house lobster, shell life, and some reef fish.

INNER BAY ISLANDS. Most of the small islands dotting the Bay of Los Angeles are easily accessible with small boats or inflatables and have good landing beaches and coves. They are characterized by generally shallow shorelines, with rock and cobblestone bottoms sloping gradually to deeper waters. These islands are best for snorkeling and shallow diving, but there is generally not a great abundance of marine life around their shallow shorelines. A notable exception is a large SUBMERGED REEF which lies between the small islands of CABEZA DE CABALLO and VENTANA.

The cool waters of the Northern Gulf house an interesting variety of colorful Dorids and Nudibranchs....always favorite subjects for macro-photographers.

This SUBMERGED REEF is located between the eastern tip of VENTANA ISLAND and the northern tip of CABEZA DE CABALLO. Visible only at low tide, the reef lies 200 yards east of the sculptured "window rock" formation on VENTANA ISLAND. The reef is comprised of a series of gigantic submerged rocks and boulders which stretch in almost single file along the backbone of a submarine ridge. Depths are shallow at the base of the large boulders, but drop off rapidly to extreme depths close on either side.

ISLA PIOJO is the outermost of the smaller island in the bay and lies slightly east of CORONADO ISLAND. Several detached rocks lie close around the projecting rocky points on the northern and eastern side of the island, providing good sportdiving locations. Depths near the shoreline drop to 30' and 40', with large rocks and boulders situated over a sandy bottom.

CALAVERAS ROCKS (also called LAS LOBERAS) is a small rounded rock whitened by bird guano. It lies approximately 1/2 mile off the southern tip of CORONADO ISLAND. A sea lion rookery inhabits the rocky reef projecting off the southeastern tip. Sportdiving is excellent around the islet, with colorful invertebrate life and an abundant fish population (gulf opaleye most common species).

Midriff Islands

The midriff islands in the Sea of Cortez situated along the Baja California peninsula coastline comprise a long, narrow chain of offshore islands that lie parallel to the coast. They are separated from the coastline by two deep channels (SALSIPUEDES channel and BALLENAS channel) that are known for their heavy tidal currents and cold-water upwellings. From north to south, they include the islands of: ANGEL DE LA GUARDA, PARTIDA, LA RAZA, ISLA SALSIPUEDES, ISLA LAS ANIMAS, and ISLA SAN LORENZO.

Diving around any of these islands is best accomplished by long range boats. Trips can be made from the Bay of Los Angeles for day excursions to some of the points within closer range of the Bay; or, the more adventuresome may go self-contained to camp on the islands. And of course, many long-range cruising boats stop over to dive the islands on their way north or south in the Cortez. At any rate, diving the midriff islands is a venture for the totally self-contained and more experienced divers only. Water rushing through the Ballenas and Salsipuedes channels during extreme lunar periods often causes tidal rips, upwellings, whirlpools and counter-currents of formidable strength around the islands, so diving should always be done with an eye out for tidal currents and any other water disturbances.

Isla Angel de La Guarda

ISLA ANGEL DE LA GUARDA (Guardian Angel Island) is the largest of the offshore islands along the Baja California coastline of the Sea of Cortez. Its barren desert surface and volcanic mountain ridges stretch 42 miles in length, with a predominantly steep and inaccessible coastline. The island lies approximately 20 miles opposite the Bay of Los Angeles. Further north, its closest proximity to the mainland is a distance of 8 miles across the deep CANAL DE BALLENAS (channel of the Whales). Good Landing Beaches are located at both the northern and southern ends of the island, as well as toward the middle of the seaward side near Ensenada Pulpito.

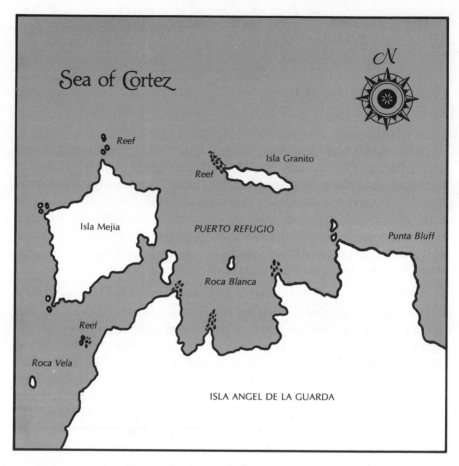

Map: Sea of Cortez showing Reef, Isla Granito, Reef, Isla Mejia, PUERTO REFUGIO, Punta Bluff, Roca Blanca, Reef, Roca Vela, ISLA ANGEL DE LA GUARDA. N (compass rose)

Puerto Refugio

PUERTO REFUGIO. Located at the northernmost end of ANGEL DE LA GUARDA is comprised of several coves backed by fine beaches and surrounded by small islands. Puerto Refugio (Refuge Harbor) is the best all-weather anchorage on the island. It is approximately 40 miles by sea from the Bay of Los Angeles.

Dark volcanic cliffs, jagged cacti and steep pinnacles combine with its tranquil waters and white beaches to create an area of breathtaking beauty and contrast. Often, when seas are rough around the island, Puerto Refugio remains placid and undisturbed. Numerous reefs and isolated rocks provide outstanding sportdiving locations in waters teeming with marine life. Puerto Refugio offers some of the best sportdiving sites round the entire island.

ISLA GRANITO is a narrow rocky island which faces the eastern side of Puerto Refugio. Several isolated rocks lie along its western shores and a fine beach occupies the eastern end of the island. A large rocky reef extending 200 yards off its northwestern tip offers a good diving location. Depths reach 50′ to 70′ along a rocky bottom, then drop abruptly to deeper waters. This reef is known for its abundance of game fish. The tiny islet is also occupied by a large colony of sea lions.

ISLA MEJIA fronts the western side of Puerto Refugio. It is separated from the main island by a small but navigable channel. Diving locations are best around the detached rocks and along the precipitous cliffs that characterize the island's circumference. A reef of submerged rocks, some partially awash, extends for nearly half a mile off the northern tip of the island in a northerly direction, dropping rapidly to greater depths on its outer edges. Visibility is usually excellent when prevailing winds subside.

PIEDRA BLANCA is the jagged white rock pinnacle located in the middle of the harbor, approximately three-quarters of a mile offshore. The steep rock has deep water close around it and drops sharply to a sandy bottom. Depths vary from 40′ to 80′. Its sheer wall surfaces are honeycombed with large crevices that house ample marine life. The sandy areas are also interesting to explore for various types of shell life. Visibility is usually good because of its location within the sheltered harbor.

THE WESTERN SHORELINE offers little in the way of protection or anchorages for boaters and divers. Steep mountain ridges plunge abruptly to deep waters with depths of over 600′ closely paralleling the coast. During extreme lunar periods, tidal currents in the Ballenas Channel reach considerable strength.

THE EASTERN SHORELINE of the island consists of a series of gravel and sand beaches with intervening rocky bluffs. Several small coves and anchorages provide protection from prevailing winds. Detached clusters of rocks signal numerous sportdiving and fishing reefs, particularly around PUNTA ROCOSA, where deep waters from the Gulf sweep in close to the point.

ISLA ESTANQUE (Pond Island), located at the southeastern tip of the Guardian Angel Island, is the closest point of shelter and anchorage on the island from the Bay of Los Angeles. A low-lying sandy point is connected to the strangely shaped ISLA ESTANQUE by a mile-long reef.

Islas Partida and Raza

The islands of PARTIDA and RAZA lie south of Angel de la Guarda island in a grouping along with several large detached rocky islets. They can both be easily reached by small boats from the Bay of Los Angeles in fair weather conditions.

PARTIDA ISLAND is a small island about 1 1/4 miles long, and 1/2 mile wide. It appears as two high plateaus of land joined together by a low, narrow strip of land. The island is made up of volcanic ash and layers of sandstone, with desert vegetation and some large cactus atop its 400-foot high peaks. Good landing beaches and anchorages lie on both the north and south side of the island. A large rock pinnacle 8 feet high is situated in a crescent-shaped cove on the northwest side of the island, and several detached rocks awash lie off the southern end. These are both excellent sportdiving locations, with marine life typical of the Bay of Los Angeles region, including lobster, scallops, sheepshead and several types of bass.

ROCA BLANCA is a large, steep rock whitened by birdlime that lies approximately 800 yards north of PARTIDA ISLAND. This is one of the best sportdiving locations near the island, with a submerged reef extending for another 700 yards northward of Roca Blanca.

RAZA ISLAND is a small, extremely low-lying island located 4 1/2 miles southeast of Partida. The shores of the island are rocky, and there are no landing beaches. A large lagoon that dries at low tide offers the only small boat entrance when the tide is high. Medium-size rocks comprise the underwater terrain immediately around the island, sloping gradually to 45' to 60'. The rocky reefs are generally barren in appearance, with reef fish, lobster and scallops in shallow depths. Schools of yellowtail come in around the island in the summer months.

The most interesting feature of Raza island is not its submarine depths, but rather the great flocks of sea birds that arrive between April and June to nest on the island. Raza island has been declared a WILDLIFE PRESERVE, and is a migratory waterfowl sanctuary. Each

HEERMANN'S GULL
Larus Heermanni

year, thousands of Heermanns gulls, Royal terns and Elegant terns, traveling from as far away as South America, begin arriving to pursue courtship rituals, establish their nests and hatch their young. At the height of the breeding season, nesting birds cover nearly every square inch of space in the large Guano-covered valleys on the island. Great flocks of sea birds wheel and soar constantly over the island to and from the sea in search of food, creating a truly spectacular sight.

Visitors are permitted on the island during nesting season, but only when accompanied by official guides. The University of Mexico maintains a small station on the island to keep vigilance during the mating season. Tern and Gull eggs are considered a great delicacy, and in the past the eggs laid by the nesting birds were harvested in such quantities by local fishermen that the bird populations suffered tremendous declines, almost certainly doomed to extinction, until the island became a preserve.

ROCA RAZA is the prominent rocky projection of a submerged peak rising 75 feet out of the water and located approximately 1 mile northwest of Isla Raza. Its sides are steep, with deep water all around. This small islet is an excellent sportdiving site, and one of the most scenic sites in the area for underwater photographers, with colorful gorgonians, sponges and fish in abundance. Its steeply sloping rock walls drop rapidly to depths of 65 to 90 feet and more within 100 feet from shore.

Salsipuedes, Animas, San Lorenzo

Continuing southward of Raza island are a long narrow chain of islands situated parallel to the coast. These are the islands of SALSIPUEDES, ANIMAS and SAN LORENZO. These islands are located at one of the narrowest sections of the Sea of Cortez, and are separated from the mainland by the deep narrow Salsipuedes channel. The southernmost and largest of the island chain, SAN LORENZO, lies only 9 miles north of SAN FRANCISQUITO BAY. Its 10-mile long volcanic surface stretches across the water like a sharp knifeblade slicing into the sea with its sheer steep sides.

The SALSIPUEDES CHANNEL (Canal de Salsipuedes) deserves mention as one of the most treacherous channels in the Sea of Cortez. Its very name, SALSIPUEDES, translates as "leave-if-you-can", giving an apt description of its turbulent nature. As the water level rises in the Gulf in response to the Pacific Ocean tides, tremendous water disturbances are created around the midriff section where these islands are located. As the rising water is funneled into the narrow, deep regions of the Salsipuedes channel, tidal streams that run with great velocity create fierce tidal rips, whirlpools, swift vortexes, upwellings and counter-currents. On an extreme lunar tide (on each full and new moon), it is wise to avoid this area in small craft, and diving should never be attempted when tidal currents are running strong. The islands in this region are recommended for experienced divers only.

There are good landing and camping beaches on all of the islands with protected coves for small boat anchorages. Numerous detached rocks, and rock pinnacles around the islands present outstanding dive spots. An outstanding diving location in this area is the prominent pinnacles located at the northwestern end of the Salsipuedes Island. Reef fish and pelagic fish swarm around these pinnacles, which are honeycombed with caves and crevices that are covered with a very colorful variety of invertebrate life.

The striped tiger anemone, often found growing on soft corals, is common in the Northern Sea of Cortez.

Sponges do not grow to great sizes in the Sea of Cortez, but the largest ones are generally found in the Northern Gulf.

To San Francisquito Bay

The coastline south of the Bay of Los Angeles provides excellent sportdiving along the cliffs and rocky outcroppings from PUNTA QUE MALO south to SAN FRANCISQUITO BAY (located 50 miles south of the Bay of Los Angeles.) This portion of the coastline lies opposite the MIDRIFF ISLANDS (so named from their location in the narrow, midriff section of the Sea of Cortez). Cold currents from the deep-water channel that lies between the coastline and the MIDRIFF ISLANDS continually bathe this rocky shoreline and headlands, providing a constant supply of nutrients to support a great abundance of marine life in this region. This portion of the coastline is exposed to prevailing winds which, along with strong tidal currents can cause rough seas for small boats. Trips by small boats and inflatables from the Bay of Los Angeles should be planned only during periods of calm weather or during the morning hours, keeping an eye out for rapid afternoon weather changes and tidal currents.

PUNTA QUE MALO is the first of the series of prominent rocky headlands along the coastline south of the bay. Several detached rocks lie close off this point, but depths close-to are generally shallow, averaging 20' to 30'. Sea lions inhabit the point. A sheltered anchorage projects inland just north of the point, providing good protection for small boats from prevailing winds.

PUNTA SOLEDAD is the next prominent point south of PUNTA QUE MALO. It can be reached easily by boat from the Bay of Los Angeles on a fair weather day. A generous scattering of gigantic boulders with sheer vertical walls surround the point, many appearing awash during low tide.

Depths around the scattering of steep boulders vary from 20' to 75' inshore, before sloping rapidly seaward. The boulders are separated by a series of sandy channels. Notable features of the area include dense growths of gorgonian corals of diverse colors, as well as a good variety of colorful nudibranchs. The exposure to all wind conditons limits visibility in the area, but averages of 30' may be expected, except in periods of extreme calm when they become greatly improved.

ISLA ROCALLOSA lies about 1/2 mile south of PUNTA SOLEDAD. It is a barren rocky islet about 75 feet high. A protected cove in the lee of the islet provides a good boat anchorage over a sandy bottom. This is a good place to take shelter from prevailing winds while diving from small boats in the area. Diving is most productive, however, on the seaward side of the island, even though this side is exposed to prevailing winds.

PUNTA LAS ANIMAS is located approximately 10 miles south of PUNTA SOLEDAD. It is an easily recognizable prominent point. The steep rocky bluff drops sharply into the sea, with depths of 80' to 100' at its base. Depths well over 400' have been charted just half a mile off the point. Currents can be severe in this area, but sportdiving is excellent. Large rock boulders with sheer walls dominate the underwater terrain. Visibility is usually much better here than at the points northward, with a greater abundance of game fish in the area, and colorful invertebrate life covering the rock walls.

FROM PUNTA LAS ANIMAS TO SAN FRANCISQUITO BAY, the shore is comprised of a series of sandy beaches interrupted by large bluffs. Several rocky islets lie close offshore, offering good sportdiving sites with prolific marine life. The game fish present in this area include yellowtail, bonito, cabrilla, grouper, jew fish, roosterfish, dolphinfish, pompano, sierra mackerel and barracuda. This portion of the coastline lies opposite the CANAL DE SALSIPUEDES, which is known for some of the most treacherous tidal currents in the Sea of Cortez. Caution should be exercised when diving and navigating in this area.

A rough dirt road, recommended for 4-wheel drive vehicles only, runs south along the coast from the Bay of Los Angeles to San Francisquito Bay. However, most of the better diving locations along this portion of the coast are accessible by boat only.

SAN FRANCISQUITO BAY (BAHIA DE SAN FRANCISQUITO) is a well protected harbor located 50 miles by sea south of the Bay of Los Angeles. It is a popular destination for cruising yachtsmen, as its sheltered harbor provides a good all-weather anchorage. It is also a popular fly-in resort destination for small planes, with a good landing strip back of the cove. It has a good supply of both aviation and marine fuel.

Tourist facilities in the area are at the present time very primitive, and include palm-thatched beach front cabins with cots, as well as beach camping sites under thatched shelters. There are restroom facilities with hot water showers, and a small resort restaurant. An isolated tropical resort atmosphere pervades, and the unique charm of this out-of-the-way harbor attracts boaters, fishermen and divers looking for a hide-away resort.

Small boats with outboard motors are available for charter with local guides for about $100/per day and $65.00/per half day. This primitive resort does cater to scuba divers, and has one of the best air compressors in the region—a 15 cubic foot 310 Ingersoll-Rand compressor. Airfills are currently around $5.00, and a limited supply of equipment rental is available.

San Francisquito Bay is a shallow, sandy basin flanked by rocky bluffs on either side. Snorkeling and scuba diving are productive around the rocky bluffs that border the bay, as well as around the rocky headlands to the north and south (including PUNTA SANTA TERESA, PUNTA SAN GABRIEL AND PUNTA SAN FRANCISQUITO). Numerous diving destinations along the coastline north and south are accessible by small boats from the Bay. Colorful semi-tropical fish such as angelfish, pufferfish and parrotfish dominate the reefs, and yellowtail come close in shore in large schools during the summer and fall months. Grouper, cabrilla and snapper are year-round residents. Lobster and scallops can also be found around the rocky reefs. The tides are less severe than those to the north, averaging 7 feet with a spring rise of 11 feet.

Chapter 5
Central
Sea of Cortez

Central
Sea of Cortez

The central region of the Sea of Cortez, extending south of San Francisquito Bay to Espiritu Santo Island just north of La Paz, offers an outstanding variety of water-recreational attractions. It is in this region that Baja's transpeninsular highway emerges from the central desert to join with the Sea of Cortez coastline at the small town of santa Rosalia, 580 miles south of Tijuana, providing coastal access along the main highway south to Loreto. For the highway traveler, the first glimpse of the Sea of Cortez is dramatic. It appears on the horizon like a shimmering pastel mirage, its aqualine surface set in stark contrast to the dusty, dry desert terrain and drab desert vegetation lining its shores.

This region of the Sea of Cortez is much more accommodating to tourists than the region to the north. There are ample facilities for fishermen, sportdivers, boaters, campers, and weekend tourists alike. Tourist accommodations range from luxury hotels to beach front campsites under charming palm-thatched huts. There are excellent sportdiving shops in Mulege and Loreto; diving tours with reliable guides and sportfishing charters can easily be arranged and are reasonably priced; and large, live-aboard charter dive boats based in La Paz run regular tours to the rich and fertile waters of this region.

The number one diving attraction of the central Gulf is its magnificent array of offshore islands. Their tranquil coves, isolated beaches and submarine gardens offer memorable pleasure to all who visit. These rugged islands are actually great chunks of granite mountains that gradually separated from the Baja mainland during a period of geological upheaval millions of years ago. Today, just their rocky summits remain above water, while their steep sides plummet into submarine depths below, providing homes for an endless variety of marine creatures.

Another outstanding water-recreational attraction in this region is the beautiful BAY OF CONCEPTION (Bahia de Concepcion). It is a long narrow bay that branches off from the Sea of Cortez between Mulege and Loreto and is entirely enclosed on three sides, appearing almost like a large inland lake. Its placid waters and white beaches have become a haven for campers, boaters, beachcombers, fishermen and divers. Trailer and RV parks as well as primitive campsites line its shores, and tiny islets lie scattered across its glassy waters.

CENTRAL GULF MARINE ENVIRONMENT

The central Gulf marine environment is more inviting to sportdivers than the northern Gulf. The tidal range is much less, averaging five feet and less, and resulting tidal currents are also not as great. The tidal currents which do arise, however, especially during the extreme lunar periods (full and new moon) are very often much too strong to swim against. Cold-water upwellings are present in the region, contributing to a rich abundance of marine flora and fauna. The rocky shoreline is steeper, providing more possibilities for beach diving locations, and creating better habitats for a more abundant concentration of marine life along the coast. The Sierra de la Giganta mountain range, towering to dramatic heights along the shoreline between Loreto and La Paz, accounts for the lack of road access into a great portion of the coastline.

The waters in this region are considered subtropical, because of the warmer winter temperatures. Winter water temperatures rarely drop below 65° F. Summer temperatures average 80° F, and can reach as high as 90° to 95° F. Because of the poor water circulation and relatively shallow depths inside the Bay of Conception, waters inside the Bay in the summertime may exceed 95° F. The cold-tolerant temperate fish-species present in the upper Gulf are largely absent in the central Gulf, although some may occasionally be seen at greater depths. The rocky coast of this region is characterized by a more tropical fish fauna, and about twice as many species of reef fish inhabit the central Gulf as the upper Gulf. The reef fish in this region are also more colorful than the often drab and cryptic species in the upper Gulf.

The protected waters around the islands and rocky shores near Loreto are noted for some of the richest habitats for reef fishes in this region. As in the upper Gulf, submarine reefs consist of submerged rock formations that vary in size and shape from underwater pinnacles to giant slabs of granite to piles of rocks scattered along a sandy bottom to more extensive rocky outcroppings honeycombed with caves and crevices. The submarine shelves around the rocky shores of most of the islands provide excellent habitats for marine life. There is less seaweed growth around the reefs than in the upper Gulf, with more varieties of soft corals and hard corals dominating the reefs. Mangrove lagoons (called "esteros") also make their first appearance in this region, playing an important part in the marine ecosystem and providing homes for several species of birds.

The region's more common reef fish include: the sergeant major, Cortez damselfish, cabrilla, two types of angelfish (King angelfish and Cortez angelfish), butterflyfish, several types of wrasses, the flag cabrilla, triggerfish, parrotfish, yellowtail surgeonfish, pufferfish, snapper, goatfish, and grunts. Moray eels, relatively uncommon in the upper Gulf, are a dominant reef resident. Three types of lobster are found in the region: Spiny Cortez lobster, the slipper lobster (called "Cucaracha" by locals, because of its curious bug-like appearance) and the red California lobster (Panulirus).

Pelagic fish also frequent the waters seasonally, and include yellowtail, roosterfish, pompano, dolphinfish, sea bass, jacks, sierra mackerel, and halibut. A great variety of shell life abounds, including scallops, oysters, several types of clams, conch, pen shells, and murex to name but a few of the more common ones. Nudibranchs, starfish, sea urchins and various anemones also lend color to the reefs. And, as in other parts of the Sea of Cortez, whales, porpoises, dolphins, manta rays, sharks, sea lions, and several species of marine birds complete the rich marine scenario.

WEATHER AND WATER CONDITIONS

With less than 4" of rainfall annually, the climate of the region is generally hot and dry. The late fall and early spring months produce milder weather, particularly when cooled by prevailing winds. Summers can become uncomfortably hot when breezes fail to appear, especially along the humid shores of Conception Bay.

DECEMBER THRU MARCH: These months produce the strongest local winds, which arise out of the north and northeast periodically, often reaching 30 to 48 knots. Water temperatures hover in the mid-60's, and sportdiving is limited by the intensity and duration of the wind conditions during these months. These winds also adversely affect water visibility, often causing it to drop below 30' during windy periods.

APRIL THRU JULY: Cool winter air and water temperatures become progressively warmer beginning mid-April, producing good diving conditions throughout the summer months with hot and dry weather. Daytime air temperatures range from 80° to 95° F, and summer water temperatures can reach 90° to 95° F, but generally average 75° to 80° F. Light, cooling winds from the northeast periodically arise in the afternoons, and winds begin to appear out of the west and southeast in July. However, the winds are not as strong or as continuous as during the winter months, and water visibilities are far better, averaging 50 to 80 feet. During the spring and summer months, water visibility can be disturbed by plankton blooms and small fry in the water.

AUGUST THRU NOVEMBER: Light winds prevail from the southeast, increasing during the afternoon hours. Southeasterlies begin to abate in October, when they give rise to the cooler, winter northeasterlies. There are few strong winds during these months, except for the appearance of gale-strength tropical storms and hurricanes (called "chubascos") which occur infrequently every few years. From mid-July to mid-September the weather is hottest and most humid, with daytime temperatures ranging from 90° to 110° F. Water visibilities are at their best during these months, and can reach as high as 100'. July through October produce the best sportdiving conditions in the region; except, of course, for the unpredictable risk of hurricanes or strong tropical storms. Two well-protected harbors in the area, Puerto Escondido and the Bay of Conception, provide storm protection for boaters in the area during these months.

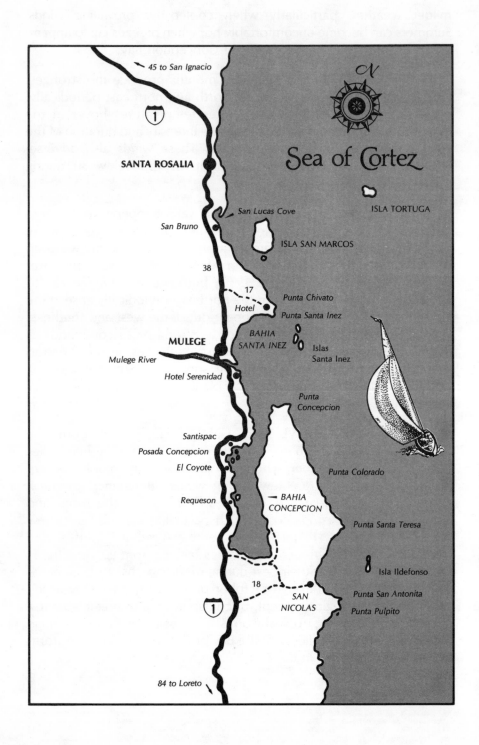

45 to San Ignacio

1

SANTA ROSALIA

Sea of Cortez

San Lucas Cove

San Bruno

ISLA TORTUGA

ISLA SAN MARCOS

38

17

Hotel

Punta Chivato

Punta Santa Inez

BAHIA
SANTA INEZ

MULEGE

Islas
Santa Inez

Mulege River

Hotel Serenidad

Punta
Concepcion

Santispac

Posada Concepcion

El Coyote

Punta Colorado

Requeson

BAHIA
CONCEPCION

Punta Santa Teresa

Isla Ildefonso

18

SAN
NICOLAS

Punta San Antonita

Punta Pulpito

1

84 to Loreto

Santa Rosalia Region

The quaint-looking town of Santa Rosalia, which resembles an old Western mining town, faces the Sea of Cortez at the point where Highway 1 emerges from the desert to follow the sea. The town of Santa Rosalia was established in the mid-1870's around a lively copper mining industry. Originally owned by the Germans, it was later purchased by the French. The mine was sold to the Mexican Government in 1954 after the major deposit of ore ran out, but the mine is still in operation today. French heritage is still evident in much of the town architecture.

TOURIST FACILITIES

Santa Rosalia is mainly an industrial town, with little or no recreational tourist facilities, other than the usual small restaurants, cafes and hotels which are part of the general make-up of the town. Gasoline, diesel fuel, grocery supplies, ice, auto parts and other general supplies are readily available. There is a small domestic airport back of the town, and postal, telegraph and international telephone service is available.

Santa Rosalia is an official port of entry for entering or exiting Mexico. Its well-enclosed artificial harbor made of mining slag is the focal point of maritime activity. Visiting yachts entering the harbor must register with the Port Captain. Regular ferryboat service operates between Santa Rosalia and Guaymas on the mainland of Mexico, accommodating both passengers, auto, and recreational vehicles.

BOAT LAUNCHING

There are no paved boat launching ramps around Santa Rosalia. Cartop or small trailerable boats may be launched over beaches in the area, with the use of 4-wheel drive vehicles. Most visitors trailering boats to Baja continue 40 miles south to Mulege to launch their boats.

DIVING

There are no facilities for sportdivers in Santa Rosalia. The closest dive shop is MULEGE DIVERS, located 40 miles south at Mulege. Many sportdivers visit diving sites along the coast between Santa Rosalia and Mulege from charter boats originating out of Mulege.

As in other parts of this region, a full wetsuit is generally needed from mid-December to mid-June, when the water temperatures are in the mid-60's. As the water becomes progressively warmer in the summer months, a wetsuit is not necessary, but it is a good idea to wear a jacket or thin wetsuit for general protection.

DIVING LOCATIONS

The beaches near Santa Rosalia itself are generally not productive for snorkeling or diving, as they are exposed to most wind conditions, have few rocky reefs inshore, and consist of barren sand or rock bottoms. Along the stretch of coastline between Santa Rosalia and Mulege lie several small offshore islands (SAN MARCOS AND SANTA INEZ ISLANDS) and the off-road region of PUNTA CHIVATO, which are both good diving locations.

ISLA SAN MARCOS (SAN MARCOS ISLAND) is a small island, about 5 1/2 miles long by 2 miles wide. It lies about a mile offshore at its southernmost end. The closest access point for small boats (car-top or inflatables) is at the small settlement of San Bruno, located 15 miles south of Santa Rosalia. Small boats can also be launched at San Lucas Cove (only 10 miles south of Santa Rosalia), where a palm-shaded cove also offers primitive beach camping sites.

At the southwest end of the island a small village of approximately 300 people center their activities around an extensive gypsum-mining industry. Limited supplies of water and gasoline may be obtained there in an emergency. A pier extends 250 yards westward of the mining town.

Both the northern and eastern shores offer good sportdiving prospects, although they do lack shelter from prevailing northerly winds. The northern point of the island is surrounded by detached rocks rising 10 to 40 feet high, with depths of 15 to 45 feet immediately surrounding. Snorkeling and diving are both excellent here, and many game fish (grouper, cabrilla, snapper) frequent the point.

Not as reclusive as some of his cousins, the Panamic green moray eel in the Sea of Cortez frequently feeds and swims boldly out in the open during the day.

ISLA TORTUGA (TURTLE ISLAND) is located 22 miles directly off the Baja California coastline, and lies about 15 mles northeastward from the northern tip of San Marcos Island. It is a solitary, oval-shaped volcanic pinnacle rising abruptly from deep waters, with a wide volcanic crater in the center and layers of sharp, dark lava rock covering its surface. There are no landings around the island, and the sharp lava rock makes shore excursions difficult. Geologists consider this island to be the youngest in the Gulf, since it appears to have erupted in a fairly recent geological era.

This steep, isolated pinnacle makes an exciting boating excursion from Mulege, where charter boats often depart for a day of diving or fishing. It is about a 2-hour boat ride from the mouth of the Mulege River, but should only be attempted when the seas are calm. The waters round the island are nearly always cold, requiring a full 1/4" wetsuit for comfortable diving, but diving is excellent along its steep, submarine ledges which are known for their large numbers of grouper and pinto bass. Depths immediately around the island drop off rapidly, and depths in the near vicinity of the island have been recorded over 5,000 feet.

PUNTA CHIVATO AREA a 17-mile long dirt road (passable with standard cars and trailers) turns off the main highway 20 miles south of Santa Rosalia and winds through the desert into the Chivato region. An abandoned hotel (possibly on the way to restoration) is located atop the bluffs overlooking Santa Inez Bay, to the right of a good dirt airstrip. Beach camping and RV sites are availabe along the water's edge in a protected cove east of the hotel. A small fee is charged, but there are presently no facilities available except restrooms and fresh drinking water. Small boats and inflatables can be launched and anchored in the protected coves between PUNTA SANTA INEZ to the south, and PUNTA CHIVATO to the north. A wide expanse of beach southwest of the hotel is excellent for shelling and snorkeling.

PUNTA SANTA INEZ lies 1/2 mile east of the abandoned Punta Chivato Hotel and is accessible by a good dirt road leading from the hotel. By sea, it is approximately 10 miles north of Mulege. There are excellent camping sites within its protected bay. Snorkeling is good along the shallow points north and south of the small bay, with a good variety of reef fish, invertebrate life and schooling fish.

PUNTA CHIVATO lies two miles north of Punta Santa Inez and is easily accessible by small boat from the beach at Punta Santa Inez. Several detached rocks lie along the North side of the point, where the bottom terrain exhibits small to medium rocky areas covered with a "sea lettuce" type seaweed, with generally shallow depths up to 40'. The scattered remains of an old shipwreck also lie strewn about at the mouth of the cove in the shallows. The west side of the point is best for snorkeling, while better diving reefs lie north and east of the point in deeper waters.

A good diving reef is located about 1/2 mile northeast of Chivato Point. A colorful reef of large rocks and boulders, with depths ranging from 30 to 90 feet at its base, is honeycombed with crevices housing scallops, lobster, brightly colored gorgonians and sea fans, cabrilla, snapper, and other reef fish. The reef meanders along the bottom like a giant wall. It is easily found with a fathometer or can be seen from the surface when the water is clear.

SANTA INEZ ISLANDS are a series of three low-lying islands, located 2 to 3 miles southeast of Punta Santa Inez, and seven miles northeast of the boat launching ramp at the Hotel Serenidad in Mulege. The waters around the islands are noted for their great abundance of fish.

MAGNIFICENT FRIGATEBIRD
Fregata magnificens

Both snorkeling and diving are best along the eastern side (Gulf side) of the islands, where submerged rocks and boulders dominate the terrain, dropping off gradually from 15' to 45' near shore, then increasing rapidly in depth within 1/4 mile east of the islands. Just two miles east of the islands, the sea bottom drops to well over 2,000 feet. The Gulf side of the islands lacks protection from prevailing winds, but marine life abounds in the shallows and at greater depths. Yellowtail, dorado and sierra mackerel seasonally frequent the islands in large numbers

The west side of the islands exhibits sandy shoal areas close to shore, with only sporadic rock outcroppings. It is generally not as productive for diving and fishing as the east side of the islands, although the waters are usually calmer and more protected. This side of the islands is a good snorkeling location.

There are a series of submerged reefs and rock pinnacles which extend out from the north end of the islands approximately one mile. They are situated along a sandy bottom in depths ranging from 60' to 90', and are excellent diving locations. Some of the rocks and pinnacles rise to within 20 feet of the surface. The shallower areas of the reefs appear barren, but at about the 50-foot depth colorful sea fans and invertebrate life appear, and schooling fish and reef fish abound. The area is open to all wind conditions and there are often strong currents in the area. These reefs can best be located with a good fathometer by heading north or northwest of the islands.

Looking over the glassy waters of Conception Bay, a popular tourist attraction in the Mulege Region.

Stretches of white sandy beaches and tranquil coves in the Mulege region attract camping and RV enthusiasts.

Mulege Region

The small town of Mulege lies 40 miles south of Santa Rosalia and is situated in a lush valley at the mouth of the Mulege River, which opens into the Sea of Cortez. Date palms, mangos, tropical fruits and flowering vines line the river banks, lending an oasis-like appearance to the otherwise dusty streets and adobe houses. Mulege is one of Baja California's oldest settlements, dating back to the first mission established in 1705. Within 600 miles driving distance from Tijuana, or just a short hop by plane, Mulege has long been a popular destination for divers and fishermen. Good sportdiving facilities and locations await visitors to the Mulege region.

TOURIST FACILITIES

A wide range of tourist accommodations is available in the Mulege area, ranging from primitive beach camping to modern RV parks to resort hotels. Some of the most beautiful beach-site camping in the Sea of Cortez is located along the serene and sandy shores of Conception Bay. Camping under the date palms along the shores of the Mulege River is also a delightful experience. Facilities available in the area include: gasoline, diesel, grocery supplies, auto parts and rapairs, boat parts and supplies, restaurants, hotels, butane, ice, and drinking water. Mulege also has a modern clinic and hospital, international telephone and telegraph services, a postal service, bus services, and a domestic airport.

BOAT LAUNCHING

Trailered boats may be launched at the paved boat ramp of the Serenidad Hotel, for a small fee. The Hotel is located at the mouth of the Mulege River on the south side. Sportfishing charters and boat rentals are also available through the hotel.

In the Bay of Conception, cartop and small trailerable boats may be launched off the beach at: Santispac beach, Posada Conception, and Coyote Beach. Larger trailerables may be launched over the sand at Posada Conception Beach, using a 4-wheel drive vehicle at high tide.

DIVING

There is a good dive shop in the town of Mulege called "Mulege Divers". MULEGE DIVERS, owned by Miguel and Claudia Quintana, is located at Calle Madero #45. Their services include: new equipment sales, a complete line of diving rental equipment (at prices comparable to the States), reliable airfills, and some equipment repairs. They also offer diving excursions from small skiffs with knowledgeable guides, for about $20.00 to 30.00 per person.

WETSUITS—Generally, a full wetsuit is necessary in the cooler winter months from mid-December thru mid-June, while summer months require only a thin wetsuit (1/8 to 3/16") or light jacket top for protection from the rock surfaces and from stinging jellyfish carried in on the currrects. Inside Conception Bay, Water temperatures warm appreciably and can reach as high as 95 F in the hot summer season. Outside the Bay, water temperatures are always slightly cooler, but can vary greatly from one location to another. Some areas continually fed by deep-water currents remain cold year-round, while others nearby warm up seasonally.

Sportdiving attractions in the Mulege area are surprisingly diverse, from the placid waters inside the Bay of Conception to the rocky headlands and islands along the Sea of Cortez coastline. Marine life tends to be more prolific outside the Bay, due to the cooler water temperatures and proximity to nutrient-rich currents. Small skiffs and inflatables are ideal for diving inside the Bay of Conception, as well as around several promontories along the coast. Diving conditions tend to be more consistent during the morning hours in this region, due to the almost year-round afternoon wind conditions. Afternoon winds can arise quickly and without warning, so small boat navigators should exercise caution.

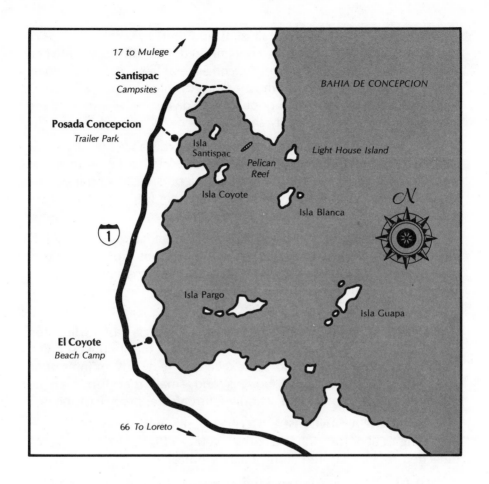

The following labels appear on the map:

17 to Mulege

Santispac
Campsites

BAHIA DE CONCEPCION

Posada Concepcion
Trailer Park

Isla
Santispac

Light House Island

Pelican
Reef

Isla Coyote

Isla Blanca

①

Isla Pargo

Isla Guapa

El Coyote
Beach Camp

66 To Loreto

The Bay of Conception

One of the most unique attractions in the Mulege area is the long, narrow BAY OF CONCEPTION (Bahia Concepcion), beginning 12 miles south of Mulege. Glassy waters dotted with small islands create miles of picturesque scenery as the main highway winds south along its shores. The entire Bay is relatively shallow, with maximum depths of 120′.

Shallow waters with depths to 30′ characterize the shorelines on both sides of the bay, except for a small portion of coastline along the southwestern shore that is inaccessible from the road. Snorkeling is popular along the shores from the beaches, but scuba diving locations within the Bay are better reached by small boats.

More than a half dozen small islets and reefs break the surface of the bay. They are generally concentrated just offshore between Santispac Lagoon and Coyote Beach. Several lie within swimming distance from the shore, but most are accessible by boat only. Small skiffs and inflatables are very popular with divers in the area, and are easy to launch over the sandy shores.

ISLA SANTISPAC lies within swimming distance of Santispac Lagoon, a popular camping cove. The island's rocky shoreline is surrounded by shallow sandy areas with depths of 20' and less. This area is best for snorkeling, with some small reef fish (sergeant majors predominate) and shell life among the rocks.

PELICAN REEF is a rocky, backbone-like reef of rocks frequently inhabited by pelicans. The rocks appear awash not more than 2 to 3 feet above the water, and they project not more than 10' below the surface to a sandy bottom. This reef is good for snorkeling and shelling.

LITE HOUSE ISLAND is the small islet marked by a flashing lite atop its rocky surface. There is a small landing beach at the southwest point. Depths around the island do not exceed 25 feet, but an interesting array of shellfish, starfish, sponges and small reef fish may be observed. Some cabrilla and schooling fish also appear occasionally.

ISLA BLANCA AND ISLA COYOTE are both snorkeling and beginning scuba locations. Depths average 15 to 30', with some detached rocks scattered along a sandy bottom.

ISLA GUAPA rises 75' above the water. It is the outermost island in the Bay, and is covered with bird guano. It has steep cliffs on its northwest face. Diving is good around the low-lying white detached rocks on the northwest side of the island, where sheer rock walls house a number of interesting caves and crevices covered with multicolored sponges, scallops, and sea fans. Some game fish, cabrilla and snapper also frequent the area.

The southwestern end of the island is characterized by large rock grottos which have been carved from the cliffs by years of exposure to the wind and water. Small boats may be anchored within their recesses, and underwater caves, crevices and large boulders lie directly beneath the surface. Depths drop to 75', sloping only gradually deeper along a sandy bottom. Large detached rocks also lie off the point, where marine life includes a variety of sponges, seafans,

The spiny red sea star is one of the most beautiful varieties of starfish found in the Sea of Cortez.

scallops, and schooling fish. This is a good area for close-up photography, but fish photography is limited.

FRIJOLI ROCK is the local name given a large submerged rock pinnacle situated near the center of Conception Bay. It is completely submerged, rising to a depth within 5' of the surface, and dropping to depths of 80' close around the rock. A good fathometer, or a local guide is usually needed to locate the rock. Marine life is more prolific here than around other islands in the Bay.

ISLA REQUESON is a low lying island to the south of the grouping of Bay islands. It is connected to the mainland by a narrow sandspit. The sandy coves on either side are popular for swimming and snorkeling. Overnight camping is allowed on the sandspit for a small fee, but there are presently minimal facilities.

To San Ildefonso Island

The coastal area continuing south outside of Conception Bay and facing the Sea of Cortez covers a 20-mile expanse of coastline. PUNTA CONCEPCION lies at the northern point, and PUNTA SANTA TERESA lies at the southern end. Accessible by boat from either Mulege or Conception Bay, this coastline is ideally suited for exploring, shelling and camping. The coastline is generally steep and rocky, interrupted by several fine beaches, coves and natural harbors. Scuba diving is excellent around the detached rocks and reefs, both awash and submerged, which extend seaward from several of the rocky outcroppings along the coast.

Generally, depths within 50 yards offshore do not exceed 80', with large rocks and boulders scattered along a sandy bottom terrain. Depths slope gradually, revealing ledges and rocky crevices that house lobster, shell life, mollusks and various species of fish, including cabrilla, sierra, snapper, grouper and tropical reef fish.

During the spring and summer months, large thickets of kelp, some of which attain lenghts of 20' and more, grow profusely around the rocky areas. Strong winds often scatter broken pieces of kelp all over the sea, reducing water visibility for sportdiving. This kelp rapidly dies off in the fall, disappearing entirely, leaving the submarine reefs better exposed to view.

PUNTA CONCEPCION lies outside the northern entrance to the Bay of Conception. Large rocks and boulders along its shoreline drop to depths of from 15' to 60'. Schools of manta rays cruise outside the reefs in the summertime, and yellowtail, marlin and dorado frequent the point seasonally.

PUNTA SANTA TERESA is a high and prominent headland with rocks awash at its base. There is a good landing beach just north of the point, and the best diving location is along the area from the point most seaward continuing to the rocks awash toward the north. Lobster, scallops, cabrilla, sierra, and tropical fish are common local reef residents.

PUNTA SANTO DOMINGO affords a protected boat anchorage in a small bight just south of the point. A shallow snorkeling reef extends westward from the beach, which is a popular shelling beach.

BAHIA DE LOS PUERCOS offers anchorage and protection from southerly winds. Diving is good along the submerged rocks around the entrance, as well as along the shoreline on the north side of the cove, where shellfish, snapper, cabrilla and schooling sierra are often found.

BAHIA SAN NICOLAS is a large semicircular bay that faces eastward to the Sea of Cortez. The bay measures 10 miles between its northern and southern extremities. Several small coves are nestled along its shoreline. A small ranching settlement is located in a lush arroyo at the southern end of the bay. San Nicolas Bay can be reached by one of two dirt roads which leave the main highway south of Conception Bay and wind along 20 miles of rough terrain into the area.

Large schools of Mexican barracuda are a common sight in the Sea of Cortez.

Some beach diving is possible along the shores of the bay, but the bay is open to prevailing winds, which generate considerable surge along the shores. Small skiffs can usually be rented from the local fishermen, who will also serve as fishing or diving guides.

PUNTA SAN ANTONITA is the first major headland to the south side of the bay. Its giant rocky headland continues underwater with large submerged rocks scattered in depths of 25 to 90 feet close around the base. This is an outstanding diving location, with colorful gorgonians and sea fans lining the faces of the large boulders, and an abundance of resident reef and schooling fish. Cold currents constantly wash around the point, creating cooler water temperatures (a 1/4" wetsuit is recommended even during the summer months), and providing nutrients for marine life.

PUNTA PULPITO lies immediately south of PUNTA SAN ANTONITA. It is a spectacular promontory, characterized by steep cliffs towering over 500 feet high. A breathtaking sight in itself, the point also harbor outstanding sportdiving waters. This area is recommended for experienced divers only, as cold waters, extreme depths, heavy currents and strong surge can create adverse conditions. Again, a 1/4" wetsuit is recommended for warmth. Cold currents bathe the point, creating thermoclines at depths below 60'. However, the cold currents foster excellent visibility, which can often exceed 100'

Depths around the point drop rapidly to 80' to 100' among large submerged boulders which lie well-concealed beneath the surface, as much as 300 yards from the point. The best diving areas are east and south of the point. Large game fish frequently sweep in around the point to feed. In addition to the great abundance of marine life in this area (lobster, cabrilla, grouper, snapper, yellowtail, jacks, shark, sierra, and dorado) this is an outstanding photo site, with extremely colorful gorgonians and hard corals providing striking contrast to the steep rock faces.

ISLA SAN ILDEFONSO is located toward the middle of San Nicolas Bay, about nine miles offshore from the fishing village at San Nicolas. It is a rocky and barren island, 1-1/2 miles long by 1/2 mile wide, belted by a steep and rocky shoreline. Jagged lava cliffs rise 400 feet above sea level, and house several species of birds. . . . blue-footed boobies, ospreys, blue herons, gulls and terns. Sea lion colonies thrive around the shoreline. There are no protected coves or landings around the island, and it is a generally unprotected dive site, open to winds and strong currents, better suited for experienced divers.

The best diving around the island is lcoated around the detached rocks on the north, south and east sides of the island. Depths around the rocks average 40' to 60', and then drop rapidly to depths over 100'. Submerged rocky reefs at both the north and south ends of the island extend seaward about 1/4 mile. Underwater terrain reveals spectacular rock pinnacles and sheer submarine rock walls covered with sea fans, gorgonian corals, hard coral and sponges. Underwater photography is outstanding anywhere along the reefs. Jewel morays and green morays are abundant, as are barberfish, king angelfish, Cortez rainbow wrasses and other tropical reef fish. The slipper lobster (which locals call "cucaracha") and spiny lobster are found around this island, and sharks, jacks and other pelagics feed around the island.

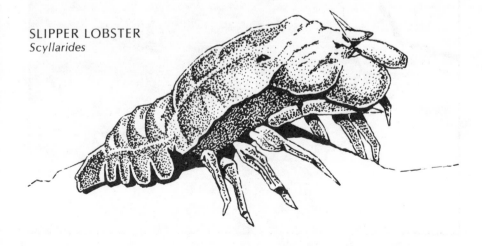

SLIPPER LOBSTER
Scyllarides

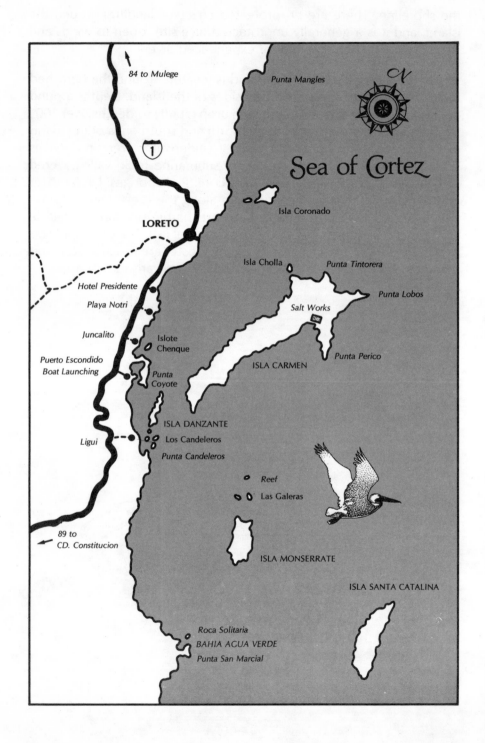

84 to Mulege

(1)

LORETO

Punta Mangles

Sea of Cortez

Isla Coronado

Isla Cholla

Punta Tintorera

Punta Lobos

Salt Works

Hotel Presidente

Playa Notri

Juncalito

Islote
Chenque

Puerto Escondido
Boat Launching

Punta
Coyote

Punta Perico

ISLA CARMEN

ISLA DANZANTE

Ligui

Los Candeleros

Punta Candeleros

Reef

Las Galeras

89 to
CD. Constitucion

ISLA MONSERRATE

ISLA SANTA CATALINA

Roca Solitaria
BAHIA AGUA VERDE
Punta San Marcial

Loreto Region

The small town of Loreto is situated 85 miles south of Mulege on Highway 1. Loreto is the home of the earliest Jesuit mission to be established on the West Coast. Founded in 1697, Loreto grew to be the largest settlement on the West coast of North America by the middle of the 1700's, only to settle into relative obscurity as the centuries rolled forward.

Today, Loreto is being "rediscovered". It is targeted for development by the Mexican government as a major center for tourism. The once sleepy town with dusty streets is now sporting streetlights and signs of modernization; resort hotels sprawl sumptuously across sandy stretches of once isolated coves; and a new, international jetport links Loreto to the outside world.

Loreto's outstanding water-recreational attractions include its miles of unexplored offshore islands and reefs; coastal waters rich in game fish and other marine life; and the beautiful all-weather harbor called Puerto Escondido (meaning "Hidden Harbor"), located 15 miles south of Loreto, where a new marina is presently under construction. Nestled against the towering peaks of the Sierra Giganta and facing the blue waters and isles of the Sea of Cortez, the Loreto region is an area of unique charm, beauty and enchantment. Although its remoteness appears destined to disappear, its scenic beauty and water recreational attractions will always lure visitors to its shores.

TOURIST FACILITIES

Tourist accommodations in the LORETO REGION range from luxury hotels to beach front camp sites. Several well established resorts in Loreto have catered to sportfishermen for many years. The newest hotel addition is the luxurious new Hotel El Presidente, located

The new marina at scenic Puerto Escondido provides good facilities and launching sites for yachtsmen and trailer boaters in the Sea of Cortez.

south of town along a beautiful cove facing the Sea of Cortez. A modern, new trailer and RV park has just been completed at Puerto Escondido, featuring hot showers, laundry rooms, and electrical hook-ups. This trailer park is ideally situated for boaters who launch their own boats into the Sea of Cortez at Puerto Escondido.

All types of facilities for tourists are available in town and include: restaurants, grocery markets, gasoline and diesel fuel, hospital and medical services, international telephone and telegraph services, postal and bus services, auto parts and repairs, fishing tackle, drinking water and ice. A new international jet airport is serviced regularly by serveral international airlines. Loreto is a natural focal point for sportdiving trips around the islands in this region, and a good dive shop in town caters to visiting sportdivers.

BOAT LAUNCHING

A concrete boat launching ramp is located at the Flying Sportsman Lodge in the south end of town. Large trailered boats can be launched into the Sea of Cortez for a small fee. Over-the-beach launching into the sea may also be attempted on several beaches south of Loreto, but 4-wheel drive vehicles are usually required, depending upon the size of the boat. Large and small trailered boats may also be launched over a firm rock and gravel ramp into the sheltered harbor at Puerto Escondido, 16 miles south of Loreto.

Boat rentals and charters are available through most of the larger tourist hotels, or through private sources at the municipal pier. The dive shop in town also offers boat charters and dive trips. Small skiffs (called "pangas") can also be rented from local fishermen along the coast, who will also serve as fishing or diving guides.

DIVING

A good dive shop called LORETO DIVERS is located at Calle Salvatierra 47. The dive shop offers diving equipment sales and rentals; reliable airfills (tank fills to 3,000 psi); and diving trips from small skiffs with local dive guides.

There is also a full-service diving and watersports operation located at the Fantasia Divers Beach Club in Loreto, next to the El Presidente Hotel . . . called Fantasia Dive. They offer airfills, rental equipment, resort courses, and diving tours from custom fiberglass dive boats. For reservations in the U.S., contact: toll-free # 1-800-336-DIVE.

WETSUITS—As at Mulege, a full wetsuit is recommended for the cooler winter months from mid-December through mid-June. During the summer months, a thin 1/8" wetsuit or jacket is recommended only for protection from the environment. Waters from Loreto southward tend to become progressively warmer in the summer time, when waters around some of the offshore islands exhibit Caribbean-like conditions.

Sportdiving in the Loreto region is mainly confined to boat diving. A few possibilities for beach diving exist in the Puerto Escondido area, but accessible shorelines generally reveal shallow and barren sand and rock bottoms. Marine life in the area is generally found in greater concentrations around the northern and eastern shores of the offshore islands where reef residents such as grouper and bass may reach tremendous sizes. This region has also long been famous for its abundant game fish populations.

DIVING LOCATIONS

Loreto to Bahia Agua Verde

ISLA CORONADO Is located 1-1/2 miles offshore, just north of Loreto, where it is easily accessible by boat from the nearby shore. A dirt road follows the coast north of Loreto for several miles, ending at a point opposite the island, where small boats can be launched over the beach.

The southwest end of the island is composed of a low-lying sandspit with a small cove, affording protection from southeasterly winds, and a good swimming and picnic beach. A shallow rocky reef extending off the point is a good snorkeling reef, dropping to greater depths several hundred yards out. The west, north and east sides of the island are comprised of steep rocky bluffs.

The northeastern and southeastern points of the island are good diving locations. Depths range from 30' to 100', and the underwater terrain reveals large rock walls and boulders interspersed with sandy area. Large game fish frequent the points. Colorful parrotfish, cabrilla, lobster and rock scallops inhabit the reefs. Some currents arise around the points, which are both open to wind and surge.

ISLOTE CHENQUE is a small rocky islet lying directly offshore from Juncalito Beach, which is located 2 miles north of Puerto Escondido. A dirt road leads into a palm-lined beach (called Juncalito) off the main highway north of Puerto Escondido. To the north of this beach in the same cove is a good sized fishing settlement. Camping, swimming and shelling are popular on this beach, but there are no facilities at present. ISLOTE CHENQUE is easily visible at the southwestern end of the cove. Small boats or inflatables can be launched over the beach.

The small island has excellent snorkeling areas on its shoreward side, and good diving locations along its northern and eastern shores. There is a small, rocky beach landing on the west side. Diving is best towards the northern end of the island, where the rocky shoreline gradually slopes underwater to depths of 70' at its northernmost point. Tropical reef fish, rock scallops, lobster, sponges, soft corals and diverse shell life abound. Halibut appear around the sandy areas in season (May, June and July), and birds nest in the cliffs atop the island.

The sandy areas along the
edges of reefs are worth exploring for dramatic photo subjects
...such as this delicate anemone
feeding in the currents.

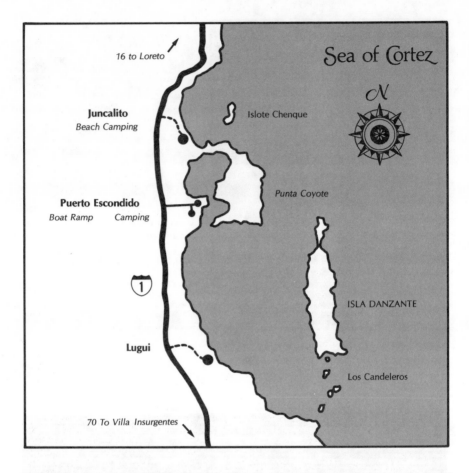

PUNTA COYOTE is located immediately northward and outside of Escondido Bay. Diving all along the length of this point is excellent and varied. Large rocks and boulders tumble down a gently sloping underwater embankment to depths of 120'-plus. Depths become shallower along the east side, where the bottom drops to 60', with intervening sandy areas. The reefs around this point are easily accessible from Puerto Escondido by small boats in calm weather, and its proximity to the sheltered harbor also makes it a recommended night diving spot.

This is an excellent spot for both wide-angle and close-up photography. Gardens of brightly colored Gorgonians and sea fans dominate the terrain at depths below 60', and colorful angelfish, pufferfish, parrotfish, triggerfish and other tropical reef fish inhabit the area.

PUERTO ESCONDIDO (Hidden Harbor) is a unique, nearly land-locked harbor, which provides refuge for boaters in all types of weather, even seasonal hurricanes. A good paved road leads west into the area from the main highway 15 miles south of Loreto. Modern RV facilities lie back of the harbor, and a new marina is under construction. This harbor is an excellent gateway to the unlimited sportdiving opportunities that lie just outside the bay among the surrounding islands. Jagged pinnacles tower high above this serene "hidden harbor" and sunsets over the glassy bay are magnificent.

ESCONDIDO BAY consists of an inner and outer bay. The inner bay is about a mile in length, with depths of 10' to 40' over a mud and sand bottom. Mangrove thickets border the large bay, and a variety of marine species enter the bay to spawn in the sheltered environment.

An outer basin, commonly referred to as the "waiting room", lies just outside the entrance channel into the bay. Depths range from 30' to 60', and snorkeling is interesting in the rocks along the shore and around the pilings of the pier, where garden eels pier out from the sand and playful schools of Mobulas (small manta rays) often congregate.

ISLA CARMEN is one of the largest islands in the Sea of Cortez, stretching 20 miles long and 7 miles wide. It lies approximately 8 1/2 miles west of Loreto, and its shortest distance to the Baja coast is about 3 1/2 miles just opposite Punta Coyote near Puerto Escondido. The island is fringed with protected bays and coves which offer good refuge from prevailing winds.

The northern region comprises the area from PUNTA TINTORERA east to PUNTA LOBOS, and then south to PUNTA PERICO. This portion of its coastline is characterized by steep, rocky bluffs with detached rocks lying close offshore around the points. The best fishing and diving locations are along the east side of the island, and around these northern promontories. A small sheltered bay, ideal for camping and day use, lies between Punta Tintorera and Punta Lobos.

Diving conditions are good around these points when the northeasterly wind conditions subside. Otherwise, moderate to strong winds can generate uncomfortable surge around the points. Depths tend to drop off sharply, and range from 50' to 150' close around the points and detached rocks. Marine life common along the reefs include: lobster, scallops, cabrilla, grouper, yellowtail, sharks, sierra, amberjack, and tropical reef fish.

The northwestern coastline of Carmen Island exhibits spectacular lava cliffs, which contain sea grottos carved into the cliffs by centuries of weather exposure. Exploring this area by boat is an exciting venture. Light reflections from the waters play continuously on the cavern walls, creating surrealistic effects. The huge cliffs drop almost vertically to the sea floor, with depths of 60' plus close to shore. This is a good diving location when southerly wind conditions disturb the rest of the island.

ISLA CHOLLA is a small islet located 1/4 mile off the northwest point of CARMEN ISLAND. The south side of the island drops to depths of 30' to 60' close to the shoreline, while the northwest side plunges to depths over 100' close around its scattered groupings of detached and submerged rocks. Colorful sea fans thrive on underwater cliffs and caves in the area, and cabrilla, grouper, yellowtail (in season) and tropical reef fish are plentiful.

ISLA DANZANTE lies 2-1/2 miles offshore at its closest point to Puerto Escondido. It is separated from the southern end of CARMEN ISLAND by a navigable channel approximately 1-1/2 miles wide. The island is more than three miles long and measures 1 mile at its widest point. Numerous detached boulders with deep water close to characterize much of the shoreline, providing varied and scenic sportdiving. The best diving locations are found along the eastern side of the island and around its southern point.

The west side of the island is comprised of small rocky bluffs alternating with sand and rocky beaches. The depths are generally shallow close in shore (10 to 35 feet), with gradual slopes to 60' over barren rock and cobblestone bottoms. It is difficult to dive on this side of the island when northerly winds arise, but snorkeling is good in calm weather, with landing beaches nearby.

TULIP SHELL
Pleuroploca princeps

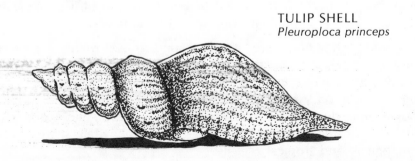

The protected waters around the islands and rocky shores near Loreto are noted for some of the richest habitats for reef fishes in the central region of the Sea of Cortez.

The northern shores of the island are dominated by steep, rocky points, with an intervening rocky shoreline. Diving around these points is excellent. Rock walls slope to depths of 80' and more. Deep canyons, crevices and submerged boulders lined with coral and sea fans provide good vistas for photography. Winds and currents can arise unexpectedly, however, generating considerable surge around the points, so due caution should be exercised.

The first large promontory on the northeastern side of the island is an excellent dive spot. Large rocks and walls slope to depths of 100' right off the point. Rock canyons lined with colorful sea fans also house lobster, scallops and reef fish. This site is open to all wind and sea conditions, and currents can arise rapidly in the nearby channel between Danzante and Carmen Island.

The southeastern side of the island contains a lower-lying coastline, with one or two sand and gravel beaches for landing ashore. Snorkeling is good along the coves and reefs in the shallows, while scattered rocks and sandy areas just offshore create good diving possibilities with depths sloping to 70' to 100'. Rock scallops, lobster and typical reef fish abound. A submerged reef extends off the southeastern point of the island near a large, detached pinnacle rock.

A sharp drop-off to 80' plus with sheer vertical walls is located on the east side of the reef. An underwater light, even during the day, is helpful in exploring the fissures and recessess of this reef.

LOS CANDELEROS (The Candlesticks) refers to three large rock pinnacles which lie between the southern point of Danzante Island and Punta Candeleros on the mainland. Spaced several hundred yards from each other and visible from Puerto Escondido, the Candeleros group are an impressive sight with their sheer, granite walls rising abruptly out of the clear, glassy waters. These rocky islets are located 5-1/2 miles southwest of Puerto Escondido and are easily accessible by boat, and both fishing and diving around these rocks is excellent.

Steep vertical walls around the three pinnacles drop sharply below the water to depths from 80' to 200'. Numerous submerged boulders lie close around the pinnacles. Looming upward from the depths, they look like the huge craggy summits of submarine mountain peaks, and create impressive underwater photo vistas. Drop-offs are dramatic, and large crevices and recesses necessitate the use of underwater lights for exploration. Large game fish frequent the area, and the site is recommended for experienced divers.

ISLA MONSERRATE lies seven miles from the nearest point of land on the coast. It is a low-lying, barren island of volcanic origin. The island is 4 miles long, and 2 miles wide, with deep water and rocky reefs close around most of its shores. There is an excellent landing beach on its northeastern shore backed by picturesque sandstone cliffs, with good snorkeling in the low-lying rocky bluffs immediately north.

Good diving locations lie just off the northern extremity of the island, which is formed by a double point and some detached rocks. Rocky ledges continue underwater around the points gradually sloping to 60' to 70' and ending in a large sandy area. Sporadic scatterings of rocky reefs interspersed with sandy areas attract tropical fish, cabrilla, snapper, scallops and shellfish.

The east side of the island is comprised of bold rocky promontories interspersed with landing coves. In several places, sunken rocky ledges with depths from 40' and 80' lie close offshore along a sandy bottom terrain, continuing 1/4 mile seaward. These reef areas can be spotted from the surface on a calm day, or with the use of a fathometer, and are excellent dive spots. They house a variety of reef and schooling fish.

At the south end of the island, rocky ledges extend into the water to form a series of finger-like rocky walls separated by long sandy channels. Snorkeling is excellent in the shallows along these rock walls, with good diving in the deeper areas as the rocky ledges slope rapidly seaward.

LAS GALERAS are two rocky islets located 2 miles north of ISLA MONSERRATE. The two islets are separated by a shallow expanse of water. They have steep granite cliff walls topped by flat, table-top plateaus. There are no landing beaches around the islets, but rocks awash on all sides provide good snorkeling in the shallows close to shore, and good diving at depths. The northeast side of the GALERAS drops rapidly to well over 100', and underwater terrain exhibits series of rock pinnacles with steep faces, and large piles of boulders that form large reef areas.

A solitary rock, protruding about 1 to 2 feet above the water lies about 1-1/4 miles northward of LAS GALERAS. This rock is surrounded by sunken rocks, with rocky reef areas extending seaward in all directions. This is an excellent dive spot, beginning in the shallows around the rock, and radiating outward.

The spiny Cortez lobster is not an important commercial species, due to the simple fact that the spiny lobster will not walk into a lobster trap in search of food, as does his cousin, the California red lobster.

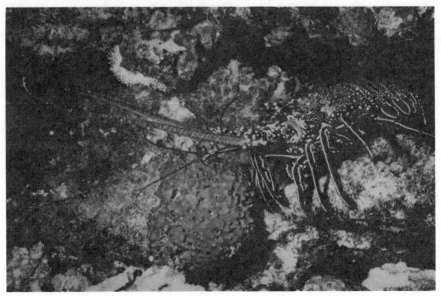

ISLA CATALAN is even more remote than Monserrate, lying 12 miles to the east of Monserrate. Catalan Island is 8 miles long and 2 miles wide. The entire shoreline of Catalan is primarily comprised of steep cliffs, only occasionally broken by beaches or coves. The eastern side of the island drops off sharply as formidable cliffs plunge steeply into deep waters at their base. The western shore is more gentle in appearance, with several small coves along its shores. This island is rarely visited by sportdiving charters, as there is little shelter from prevailing winds anywhere around the island.

However, when seas are calm around the island it is possible to anchor in either of the large coves located along the southwest and southeast tip of the island, where there are good landing beaches for hiking ashore. The steep rocky points and detached rock pinnacles that fringe the edges of the coves are excellent diving locations. Snorkeling is also good in the shallows along the inside edges of the coves.

The drop-offs along the rocky points are dramatic, with sheer rock walls plunging almost vertically to depths of 70' to 90' along their bases. The submarine terrain is dominated by giant boulders and rock walls lined with deep crevices. The rock surfaces are generally lacking in invertebrate life in the shallower depths, but reef fish are abundant, including large parrotfish, triggerfish and angelfish. At depths below 80', large gardens of sea fans and gorgonian corals appear around isolated rocky outcroppings at the base of the rocks. Pelagic game fish are abundant in the area, along with occasional sharks and manta rays.

Catalan Island is home to two unusual life forms on the island. The only species of rattleless rattle snake in the world is confined to this tiny island. Its venom is extremely poisonous, so due caution should be exercised when hiking on the island. A unique species of giant barrel cactus also grows on the desolate slopes of the island, many specimens reaching a height of ten feet with a diameter exceeding three feet.

BAHIA AGUA VERDE (The Bay of Green Water) is a large, scenic protected bay situated along the Baja coastline about 100 miles southeast of Mulege. This bay lies in the inaccessible region of the Cortez between Loreto and La Paz at the base of the Sierra Giganta Mountain range. Palm trees and tropical shrubs grow profusely along the shore, and a small fishing village that also raises goats is located

BROWN BOOBY
Sula Leucogaster

back of the shore, where fresh water and limited supplies can be obtained. A small trail runs from the village to a dirt road connecting to Loreto farther north.

The Agua Verde Bay is tucked in a bight between two prominent points of land, and is actually comprised of 5 small coves within the larger one, with some prominent rock pinnacles isolated near the shore in the area. Some rocks awash and submerged reefs extend out from the southern point of the bay to PUNTA SAN MARCIAL, which lies 2-1/2 miles east of Agua Verde Bay. A good diving area is located at ROCA SOLITARIA, a large white needle-shaped pinnacle lying 600 yards off the northern point of the bay. The pinnacle drops to depths of 60' to 120' close to, with submerged rocks and boulders scattered around the area. The reefs around this rock are frequently fished by local fisherman.

PUNTA SAN MARCIAL is a high bluff of land 2-1/2 miles west of Agua Verde Bay. Numerous detached rocks lie close around its shore, with submerged reefs extending seaward for several hundred yards from both its northern and southern points. The best diving location is along the reef extending for 1,200 yards off the southern point. The top of the reef exhibits large bare boulders, and the outside edges of the reef drop to depths of 60' to 90' over a sandy bottom. Sea fans, lobster, scallops, tropical fish (angels, butterflyfish, parrotfish), cabrilla, and schooling reef fish inhabit the reef, and large schools of sierra, yellowtail, jacks and tuna make seasonal appearances.

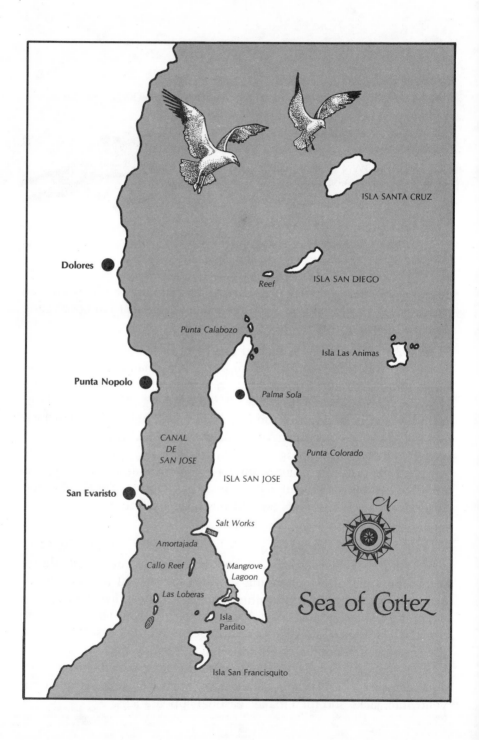

ISLA SANTA CRUZ

Dolores

Reef

ISLA SAN DIEGO

Punta Calabozo

Isla Las Animas

Punta Nopolo

Palma Sola

CANAL
DE
SAN JOSE

Punta Colorado

ISLA SAN JOSE

San Evaristo

Salt Works

Amortajada

Callo Reef

Mangrove
Lagoon

Sea of Cortez

Las Loberas

Isla
Pardito

Isla San Francisquito

San Jose Island Region

The San Jose Island region, located midway between Loreto and La Paz, is one of the most inaccessible coastal regions in the Sea of Cortez. Rugged mountain peaks, part of the towering Sierra de la Giganta, rise from the shoreline without interruption for miles along the coast, reaching skyward more than 5,000 feet in some places. Primitive burro trails zig-zag the mountainsides, providing vital links between the high sierra villages and the island dwellers below. Sunsets that splash across these mountain pinnacles in blazing colors cast a fiery glow upon the waters below, giving a primordial atmosphere to this enchanting and remote region.

The local residents of the area use small skiffs (called pangas) with outboard motors as their sole means of transportation, and frequently make the trip by boat to La Paz, some 60 miles away, for supplies. Many of the inhabitants of the region are descendents of the hardy "Vagabundos del Mar", who roamed the Sea of Cortez in wooden canoes with tattered sails. Today, they venture forth in small skiffs (now fiberglass) to fish the reefs of the Cortez much the same way their ancestors did generations ago. Locals still tell tales of hand-harpooning large sharks alongside small canoes, and free-diving to great depths for pearl oysters during the pearling era.

Long range boats cruising the Sea of Cortez often stop at a popular anchorage on the island of San Francisquito, which has a well-protected perfectly half-moon shaped bay. There is a large evaporative salt works on the south end of San Jose Island, which generates frequent boat traffic to and from La Paz for supplies and provisions. Good camping beaches and landing coves can be found on most of the islands in the region; and fresh water is sometimes available from local sources.

This region has some of the most outstanding diving attractions in the entire Sea of Cortez. Magnificent beaches, sheltered coves and abundant marine life surround the islands, and rocky pinnacles and submerged reefs protrude from the deep, clear waters nearby. Chater dive boat operations radiating from La Paz head northward into this region to explore its almost limitless diving possibilities, cruising from island to island as their passengers enjoy diving on a wide variety of submarine reefs along the way. Some of the charter boats make regular trips between Loreto and La Paz throughout this region. The larger islands in the region include the islands of: Santa Cruz, San Diego, San Jose and San Frncisquito.

ISLA SANTA CRUZ is the northernmost of this group of islands. It is a barren granite land mass that rises abruptly from deep waters to a maximum height of 1,500 feet. Its shoreline is dominated by sheer, steep cliffs. The eastern side of the island is totally inaccessible, rising almost perpendicular from the sea. There is only one small landing beach on the island, located on the southwestern end of the island. The best diving location is along the northern point of the island. At the north end, the rocky shoreline drops off quickly to reveal a submarine terrain covered with medium and large boulders. The huge rocks slope downward underwater at a 45° angle, ending in a flat sandy ocean floor at a depth of 110 feet. The rocks are thick with reef fish in the shallower depths, and are covered with sporadic growths of colorful sea fans. Large groupers and cabrilla cruise along the deeper areas where the rocks meet the sand. Giant manta rays are also often seen cruising around this shoreline.

ISLA SAN DIEGO lies about 3-1/2 miles south of Santa Cruz Island, and is a popular diving destination, with both shallow and deeper reefs in its vicinity. The small island is barely 1 mile long, and is a barren volcanic ridge. It has steep rocky cliffs along its northeastern side, but its southwestern shore has a gentler slope and a gravel beach along its shoreline that affords good access to the island. Detached rocks lie around the northeast and southeast points.

The west side of the island has detached rocks along the shoreline which extend about 50 yards seaward. Snorkeling and diving along this shore reveal large boulders scattered over a sandy bottom with depths from 30' to 60'. Particularly dominant are giant, brilliantly patterned parrotfish and large numbers of surgeonfish and Cortez damselfish.

A diver pauses to examine the great variety of invertebrate life that thrives along rocky reefs in the waters around Baja's offshore islands.

The north and east shore of the island consists of large boulders, both submerged and awash, with depths close inshore dropping off from 30' to 70'. The rocks are somewhat barren in appearance, locking in invertebrate life and color, but fish watching and fish photography are excellent, with a great variety of tropical reef fish in the area.

SAN DIEGITO REEF is the name locals have given the group of large detached rocks awash several hundred yards southwest of the island. Snorkeling and diving is excellent around the rocks awash, with immediate depths to 45' over a sandy bottom. The rocks are honeycombed with scenic caves whose enrances are framed with multicolored sea fans. Extending 1/2 mile eastward from the rocks awash is a large underwater wall which peaks to within 5' of the surface and drops to a depth of 45'. This long, rocky wall houses sponges, scallops, gorgonian corals and sea fans and colorful reef fish.

San Diegito reef is a spectacular photography site, and tropical butterflyfish, angelfish, surgeonfish, parrotfish, pufferfish, and brilliant starfish also lend color to the reefs. Medium to large boulders extend 1/4 mile south of the reef with shallow depths prevailing. The bottom terrain around SAN DIEGITO REEF exhibits low-lying rocky ledges, interspersed with sandy areas.

LAS ANIMAS is the name of the most seaward group of rocky pinnacles in the San Jose Island region. Located nine miles directly east of San Jose Island, Las Animas is a small steep rock island that rises abruptly from deep waters, with several smaller detached pinnacles around its circumference. Sheer walls on all sides drop off to depths of 300' and more close inshore, and depths of 3,000' have been sounded within 1/4 mile of the island. This small island is considered one of the best dive sites in the Sea of Cortez.

Diving around the entire Las Animas shoreline as well as around its detached rocks reveals a great variety of spectacular submarine terrain including large caves, rock crevices, giant boulders, steep pinnacles, sheer walls and rocky ledges covered with gardens of giant sea fans. Cold waters from deep basins are continually brought to the surface by currents and upwellings, which maintain cool water temperatures and generally good underwater visibility, as well as a superabundance of marine life. Large schools of reef fish swim among the sea gardens, and divers never know what to expect next at this marine feeding station. Black marlin, manta rays, hammerhead sharks, dorado, yellowtail, jacks, pompano, sea turtles and large grouper have all been spotted by divers in the area.

Diving at Las Animas is recommended for experienced divers. Hazards include strong currents, extreme depths, open-ocean conditions and rapid weather changes. There is no well-protected anchorage, but locals anchor in a small bight on the southwest end in depths of 100', while also tying their stern lines off to the rocks on shore, and with an eye open to changing wind conditions.

ISLA SAN JOSE is the largest island in the area, measuring 16 miles long and 4 miles wide. A large evaporative salt works is located on the southwestern end of the island, and a small fishing village lies along its northeastern shore. The island appears to be barren, but it is considered one of the most fertile islands in the Gulf and several species of wildlife occupy its rugged and mountainous interior, including goats, deer and coyote as well as rattlesnakes and rodents.

Las Animas pinnacles typically reveal very steep submarine cliffs and rock faces thickly carpeted with soft corals.

A California male sea lion.... undisputed king of the sea lion rookery at Las Animas.

A large mangrove lagoon occupying over 1,000 acres is located at the southeast end of the island, with an easily visible small boat entrance facing west directly opposite CAYO REEF. Edible oysters grow on the mangrove roots, and several species of clams are buried in the mud flats near its entrance. Due to the still and humid waters of the mangrove swamp,which provide an ideal insect breeding site, the area is infested with a bothersome species of biting gnat called JEJENES, (or NOSEEUMS) during the spring and hot summer months. This lagoon is one of the most beautiful mangrove lagoons in the Sea of Cortez, attracting a myriad of exotic birds, including frigate birds, herons, and egrets.

THE WEST SIDE OF SAN JOSE ISLAND lies parallel to the coastline across the deep San Jose Channel. The shores are low-lying with sporadic sand and rock beaches backed by dense desert undergrowth. Although there are several bays and good anchorages located along this side of the island, there are few good diving reefs along the shore and this coastline (north of Punta Salinas) is rarely visited by sportdiving charters. Geneally, barren rock and cobblestone shelves slope steeply into the channel.

PUNTA CALABOZO is the northern extremity of SAN JOSE ISLAND. Diving around its steep, dark-colored rocky bluffs and detached rocks reveals large boulders scattered sporadically along a sandy bottom in depths from 30' to 60', with some large caves in the area. Gorgonian and hard coral growth is sporadic on the rocks. A reef of rocks, some protruding above water, extends 1/4 mile off this point and is frequented by cabrilla, grouper, triggerfish, sierra, schooling reef fish and seasonal game fish (yellowtail and dorado). Natives dive for conch seasonally in the sandy areas around the point.

PUNTA COLORADO (Red Point) is the easternmost point of land on the island. Diving and snorkeling are good around the rocky ledges that project from the coastline. These ledges sprawl along a sandy ocean bottom, dropping to depths of 5' to 50'. Continuing south from Punta Colorado along the coast is one of the most scenic areas on the island. A small bay just south of Punta Colorado is comprised of spectacular red rock and sandstone eroded cliff formations framing stretches of pristine, white sand in a series of finger-like coves. The landing beaches are excellent, and the shallow rocky ledges are good snorkeling areas.

The mangrove lagoon on San Jose Island, which often attracts such exotic species of birds as egrets and herons, is an interesting place for a side trip between dives.

THE EAST SIDE OF SAN JOSE ISLAND is comprised of a series of high rocky bluffs dropping off steeply into the sea and intespersed with sand beaches. Diving is good anywhere along the prominent rocky bluffs on this side of the island, with depths varying from 30' to over 100' close inshore. Colorful reef fish abound, and lobster and game fish are plentiful.

BAHIA AMORTAJADA is a large bight tucked into the southwest corner of San Jose Island immediately in front of the saltworks settlement, between PUNTA SALINAS AND PUNTA OSTIONES. Boats often anchor here for protection from southerly wind conditins, and the long stretch of sandy beach fronting the bay is an excellent shelling and beachcombing site, (except for the hot summer months when the JEJENES are fearsome). Natives often dive for conch in the sandy depths just off the beach. The name AMORTAJADA, meaning sleeping mummy, derives from the sculptured hills back of Punta Salinas, which from a distance resemble the figure of a sleeping female mummy.

A good area for shallow diving (depths to 60') and snorkeling lies along the west side of Punta Salinas parallel to the San Jose Channel. A rocky shoreline continues underwater with small to medium-sized rocks fringing the point and ending along a sandy bottom in depths of 60' about 50 yards offshore. Lobster, scallops, cabrilla and reef fish dominate the reef, but the site is open to all wind conditions and currents that arise in the San Jose Channel.

CAYO REEF is a narrow backbone ridge of boulders about 1/4 miles long that is located at the south end of AMORTAJADA BAY near the Mangrove Lagoon. The ridge projects from 10' to 40' above the surface, and is covered with white birdlime and inhabited by birds. The word "cayo" (also spelled "callo") is the native word for the large rock scallop found in the area. CAYO REEF is a popular diving location within easy distance from a comfortable anchorage. Its eastern side is very shallow, with large boulders dropping abruptly to meet a sandy bottom at a depth of 30'. Pen shells, clams and scallops are often found along this side of the reef, and colonies of serpentine-like Cortez garden eels can be observed in the sandy areas.

The western side of CAYO REEF permits deeper diving, as large detached rocks drop to immediate depths of 20' to 60' feet, ending in a sandy bottom. This area generally lacks colorful scenery for photography, but fish life is more abundant, particularly cabrilla and other schooling fish. This side of the reef is open to currents and prevailing wind conditions.

ISLA PARDITO is a small, barren island resembling nothing more than a large, 40-foot high rock protruding from the sea. It is densely inhabited by several families of fishermen, who have been fishing the waters of the Cortez for several generations. There is no fresh water source on the rock island, and consequently no crops or vegatation on its barren surface. All supplies are periodically brought to the island from La Paz. Many detached rocks rise from the waters around the islet in usually shallow depths of 30' and less. The island inhabitants welcome visitors, but it is best to ask their permission before diving around their "front yard".

ROCA LA REINA (Queen Rock) is an interesting diving site located just north of PARDITO ISLAND. It is a solitary pyramid-shaped rock that protrudes barely 5' above the surface of the sea, extending underwater in a cone-shaped formation of large rocks and boulders situated over a sandy ocean floor in depths of 50'. Its name is well-deserving, because of its regal submarine decor. Gigantic red and orange sea fans line rocky crevices which house myriads of colorful reef fish, including angelfish, snapper, butterflyfish, and triggerfish. Fish photography is excellent in the area, but strong currents often arise rapidly around the rock, and wind chop can easily disturb visibility.

ISLA SAN FRANCISQUITO is a small hilly island of volcanic lava lying to the south of San Jose Island. It has an excellent, crescent-shaped anchorage on its southwestern shore, called BAHIA SAN FRANCISQUITO, where boats in the area often seek refuge from local hurricanes and tropical storms. A long, white sandy beach is noted for the tiny "pookah" shells that wash up on its shore. JEJENES and mosquitos can be very fierce in the summer months when the winds abate in this anchorage. It is uninhabited, except for occasional local fishermen, and sometimes residents in the area keep small herds of goats on the island. Excellent dive spots around the island are located at the south end of the island, and midway along the eastern shore.

The south end of the island has a rocky shoreline with large, detached boulders dropping to depths around 80' close inshore. The otherwise barren boulders have sporadic coral growths in caves and crevices, and lobster, tropical reef fish, and bold moray eels are the dominant residents. Schooling and seasonal game fish periodically sweep in around the point.

The Sea of Cortez, one of the most fertile bodies of water in the world, is known for its large numbers of schooling pelagic and reef fish.

Midway along the eastern side of the island are a series of rocky ledges extending from shore at several points along the coastline. The diving is shallower here, with depths prevailing from 30' to 50',but several caves and large detached boulders house colorful sea fan clusters and a good number of tropical reef fish.

LAS LOBERAS is a rocky ridge comprised of two flat rocks situated 2 miles northwest of ISLA SAN FRANCISQUITO. The rocks are inhabited by birds and sea lions and several detached sunken boulders lie in their immediate vicinity in depths of 30' to 60' along a sandy ocean floor. Diving around the rocks themselves is excellent, but the area is open to currents and winds, and visibility is limited when currents are running.

A large submerged rocky reef extends out 3/4 mile southwest from the south end of LAS LOBERAS. The shallowest point of this submerged reef area surfaces to within 15 feet, and can be located by a fathometer. It is also quite visible from the surface on a calm day and comprises a large reef area dominated by rocky ridges and boulders, that are abundant with gorgonians, hard corals, colorful reef fish (angelfish, butterflyfish, pufferfish, triggerfish), cabrilla, snapper and schooling fish. Sea turtles and sharks also frequent the reefs, and the area is an excellent photo site.

Chapter 6
Southern
Sea of Cortez

Southern Sea of Cortez

The southernmost portion of the Sea of Cortez encompasses the waters surrounding the beautiful La Paz Harbor and continuing southward to Cabo San Lucas. The Sea of Cortez waters merge with the Pacific Ocean at Cabo San lucas where the Baja California peninsula terminates abruptly in a ridge of jagged rock pinnacles that plunge dramatically into the sea. This region boasts a coastline of unsurpassed beauty, with stretches of white, sandy beaches scattered generously along the coastline, and breathtaking luxury hotels sprawling sumptuously across tranquil coves shaded by lush tropical palms.

It is in this region that the term "tropical paradise" most closely materializes in the arid, desert peninsula of Baja California. Palm-lined restaurants facing the crystalline waters of the Sea of Cortez serve up tempting dishes of fresh local seafood while patrons enjoy a refreshing "cerveza" or a Mexican "margarita" or simply a relaxed chat in the fresh ocean breeze. It is no wonder then that this region offers more resorts and facilities for the tourist than any other part of Baja California. The large and bustling town of La Paz, once a sleepy and dusty pueblo, has exploded with growth during the last decade. It now offers most facilities found in any modern city in the world, but it has still managed to retain its sleepy, small-town charm and relaxed atmosphere as it stretches lazily along a picturesque palm-lined harbor. La Paz is the largest port of entry into Mexico along the Baja coastline in the Sea of Cortez. Most cruising yachts always stop here for supplies, provisions and a taste of civilization.

Hotels in the Cape Region are noted for their charm and beauty.

The once isolated Cape region around Cabo San Lucas has also burgeoned with construction, but architecture in the region is aesthetic and well-planned, enhancing and blending with the natural beauty of the region. Resorts in the Cape region are famous for their architectural standards of beauty and charm. A new international jet airport is situated at San Jose del Cabo, and a road along the coastline from Cabo San Lucas to Cabo Pulmo and then inland to La Paz is undergoing rapid improvement, opening up a previously inaccessible stretch of coastline along the shores of the Cape region.

The waters in the southern Gulf region hold a remarkable variety of attractions for sportdiving enthusiasts. Several large charter dive boats operate out of La Paz, visiting the waters surrounding La Paz as well as the waters to the north and south along the coast. Beach diving and diving from small skiffs is excellent at underwater reefs all along the coast, and the region holds several unique diving attractions, including: the Cabo Pulmo coral reef—the only living coral reef on the West Coast of North America; the famous underwater "sand falls" in the submarine canyon at San Lucas Bay; a giant underwater seamountain frequented by friendly manta rays, immortalized in a novel by Peter Benchley; and the submerged Gorda Banks, where mammoth whale sharks often allow contact with divers.

SOUTHERN GULF MARINE ENVIRONMENT

The southern Gulf marine environment exhibits less seasonal fluctuations than any other part of the Gulf. Onshore water temperatures can vary from 68° to 90° F, but usually stay between 75° and 85° F. The warmest surface waters are located in the Cabo San Lucas area, where water temperatures range from 72° to 95° F. The waters are generally warmest between the late spring and early fall months, and the months from June through October produce the most consistently good diving conditions in the region. The tidal range also exhibits the least movement in this southern region, ranging from 3' to 5', but can produce currents of surprising strength, especially around the offshore islands and in the channels between the islands and the mainland.

The marine flora and fauna of the southern Gulf region between La Paz and Cabo San Lucas is typically subtropical to tropical, due to the warmer winter sea temperatures. The coastal area between La Paz and Cabo San Lucas contains some of the richest reef fish fauna in the Sea of Cortez. The coastal terrain exhibits steeper shorelines and clearer waters than elsewhere in the Gulf, and the coast is characterized by large areas of rocky tide pools rich with marine life. Diverse types of shorelines in the area, ranging from sandy beaches to mangrove swamps to rocky headlands also contribute to producing a rich mixture of shore fish. Typical reef fish in the region include: pufferfish, cornetfish, triggerfish, surgeonfish, porkfish, parrotfish, angelfish, cabrilla, grouper, snapper, sergeant majors, butterflyfish, wrasses, damselfish, goatfish, and barberfish—to name only the most common.

Reef structures in the southern Gulf region are typical of those throughout the Sea of Cortez, being mainly comprised of large rocks and boulders, rock walls, submarine canyons, submerged volcanic ridges and rocky backbones and ledges situated over sandy ocean floors. The only exception is the unique coral reef at CABO PULMO, which is comprised of profuse coral colonies (Pocillopora capitata) growing on dikes of extruded igneous rock, supporting a species-rich coral reef community. Submarine reefs in the southern Gulf region attract a greater number of more colorful species of marine flora and fauna (such as the Panamic porkfish, blue and gold snapper, Clarion angelfish and Pacific boxfish) as well as a greater abundance of those tropical fish species also found in the central Gulf region (including the barberfish, Mexican goatfish, beaubrummel damselfish, coral hawkfish, and the orangeside triggerfish).

Sporadic isolated growths of stony corals are found in greater abundance along the reefs in this region, along with the usual varieties of sea fans and gorgonians also occuring in the central Gulf region. The yellow colonial TUBASTREA corals are especially dominant along the

Reefs in the Cape Region are often thickly carpeted with bright orange Tubastrae coral.

reefs, and are usually most abundant on the underside of large overhangs and crevices. This coral also occurs in the central Gulf region, though not as profusely.

An interesting variety of shell life flourishes along the coastline. Rock scallops, pen shells, oysters, pearl oysters, clams, conch and murex are typical of the region. Large game fish frequent the waters seasonally, and include yellowtail, marlin, roosterfish, dolphinfish, tuna, amberjack, snapper, sierra mackerel and barracuda. And of course, the southern Gulf region also has its share of cetaceans, manta rays, sharks, sea lions and marine birds. An interesting seasonal visitor in the region is the mammoth whale shark, which can be seen basking occasionally in the warm surface waters off the coast.

WEATHER AND WATER CONDITIONS

The La Paz region presents a typical desert terrain, covered with dry brush and cactus; but what would be an otherwise hot and dry desert is cooled almost year-round by light breezes which create a mild and comfortable climate. The humidity is low, and the annual rainfall is four inches or less. The Cape Region (extending from Cabo Pulmo to Cabo San Lucas) is located in the tropics, but the climate is generally also hot and dry. The weather along this section of the coast is considered to be the mildest of the entire Baja California peninsula. Year-round diving is possible, and is limited only by the intensity and duration of the prevailing winds, which tend to be stronger during the winter and early spring months.

NOVEMBER THRU MARCH: These months are considered the "winter season" for diving, but daytime temperatures are mild (from 70° to 90° F) and more comfortable than in the hot summer months. Light northwesterly winds generally prevail, arising in the morning and often continuing through the late afternoon. Toward the spring months, in the La Paz region, these winds can be accompanied by southeasterly winds which last the duration of the night, and can be quite intense. Water visibility is reduced during these months (20′ to 30′), espeically when strong winds blow for several days. Diving conditions can be sporadically good, but are not consistent.

APRIL THRU JULY: Winds from the southeast and southwest prevail, arising in the late afternoon and cooling the otherwise hot afternoons and providing mild evenings. The southerly winds (locally called the COROMUELS) generally blow steadily through the night and subside by mid-morning. Diving conditions are sporadically good from April thru May, and begin to be more consistently good in June and July, with water visibilities averaging 50' to 70' as winds become lighter and waters become warmer. More frequent periods of prolonged calm weather begin to appear in April, and diving conditions are largely dependent upon the strength and duration of the prevailing winds. From mid-June onward, diving conditions improve steadily, and are consistently good from mid-July through mid-October.

AUGUST THRU OCTOBER: These months (along with July) produce the best conditions for diving. However, daytime temperatures can be uncomfortably hot and tropical storms often create high humidity. Generally, winds prevail from the south in the mornings and afternoons, then change around to the west in the late afternoon and evenings. Sportdiving conditions are predictably good during these months, and diving conditions are optimum during periods of prolonged calm weather, with water visibilities often exceeding 100', and water temperatures in the high 80's and 90's. However, this is also the season for the appearance of local hurricanes (called CHUBASCOS) and tropical storms, which occur only every few years, but can reach devastating strengths and are unpredictable in their appearance. The chance of tropical storms decreases in October, and diving conditions often remain consistently good thru November.

SPINY OYSTER
Spondulis princeps

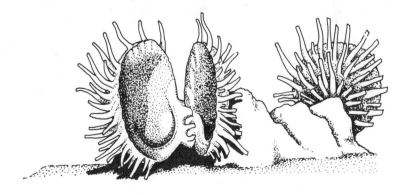

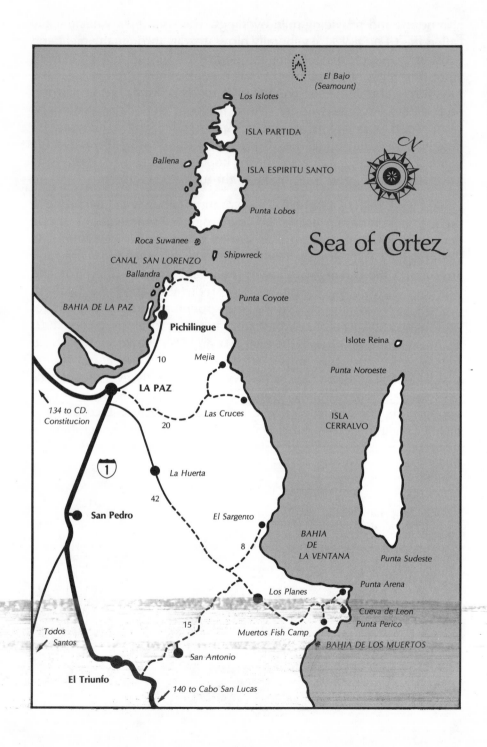

El Bajo
(Seamount)

Los Islotes

ISLA PARTIDA

Ballena

ISLA ESPIRITU SANTO

Punta Lobos

Roca Suwanee

Sea of Cortez

CANAL SAN LORENZO   Shipwreck

Ballandra

Punta Coyote

BAHIA DE LA PAZ

Pichilingue

Islote Reina

10   Mejia

Punta Noroeste

LA PAZ

134 to CD.
Constitucion   20   Las Cruces

ISLA
CERRALVO

1

La Huerta

42

San Pedro   El Sargento

BAHIA
DE
LA VENTANA

8

Punta Sudeste

Los Planes   Punta Arena

Cueva de Leon
Punta Perico

Todos
Santos   15   Muertos Fish Camp

BAHIA DE LOS MUERTOS

San Antonio

El Triunfo   140 to Cabo San Lucas

158

la Paz Region

Situated slightly north of the Tropic of Cancer in the lower portion of the Sea of Cortez, the waters surrounding the city of La Paz (meaning the "city of peace") have enjoyed great popularity with both past and present day mariners. The history of the area is rich in nautical adventure and pirate lore. La Paz was discovered in 1533 by a Spanish expedition sent out to explore the fabulous "Isle of Santa Cruz" (the name given Baja at that time, which was believed to be an island). This mythical "Santa Cruz" island was rumored to be the stronghold of a race of Amazon women rich in Aztec gold and pearls.

Subsequent expeditions to the region dispelled the myth, and the tales of Amazon women and gold proved unfounded. But the tales of pearl treasure proved to be true. Pearls were a much coveted commodity in Mexico at that time, and La Paz gained quick renown as rumors of its fabulous pearl wealth spread. Adventurers, pirates and treasure-seekers soon flocked to its shores. Rich beds of pearl oysters were abundant everywhere in the fertile waters of the region, and La Paz became the center of colonization, pirateering and pearling activities for the next 400 years.

In the late 1930's a mysterious plague suddenly devastated all of the rich, pearl oyster beds in the region, bringing an abrupt halt to the pearling activites. Native rumors whisper that the pearl beds were actually poisoned by foreign concerns in the region anxious to eliminate competition for the newly developed synthetic pearls. But no one really knows exactly why the great pearl beds disappeared so suddenly. It is also quite possible that they may have been simply over-harvested to the point of exhaustion or extinction, as has frequently happened in history with so many rich resources of the past.

With its major source of income depleted, La Paz began turning its energies to domestic concerns . . . the needs of its growing population and a steadily increasing influx of tourists seeking respite and recreation along the shores of the "City of Peace."

TOURIST FACILITIES

Today, La Paz is the capital and largest city in the southern state of Baja California, and is a busy center of maritime activity. The lively city of La Paz offers modern and attractive tourist accommodations along the palm-lined shores of a beautiful natural harbor. Charming hotels with seaside pools, open-air restaurants, modern RV and trailer parks, native markets, and recreational facilities cater to a variety of tourist needs and interests. Modern supermarkets, nightclubs, discoteques and even pizza parlors now lend a cosmopolitan atmostphere to this once sleepy village. A large international airport services the city; bus routes connect to other parts of Baja; a modern ferry terminal located east of town in Pichilingue Bay connects Baja with Topolobampo and Mazatlan; and the city offers good international communication facilities and modern medical services.

The La Paz Bay is the largest body of protected water in the Sea of Cortez, and is always populated with cruising yachts and sailboats. Its sheltered harbor and modern conveniences make La Paz an ideal gateway to the region's beaches, coves and offshore islands in the surrounding waters of the Sea of Cortez. Fishing and diving charters can easily be arranged through the larger tourist hotels in the city, and several large and comfortable charter dive boats make regular cruises from the harbor with groups of diving enthusiasts from all over the world. La Paz is the most popular center of diving activities in the Sea of Cortez, ideally situated within easy access of some of the most beautiful diving the Sea of Cortez has to offer.

BOAT LAUNCHING

Large trailered boats may be launched into the La Paz Bay. A ramp is located in the boatyard near the old ferry terminal on the beach just south of town, near Calle Sinaloa. A small fee may be required.

Small trailered boats and car-tops may be launched from a public beach near La Posada Hotel, to the north of town. The Pichilingue

The city of La Paz, which is the capitol of the state of Southern Baja (Baja California Sur), faces a beautiful palm-lined harbor.

public beach, 11 miles north of town near the ferry terminal, also affords over-the-beach launching for small boats and inflatables.

DIVING

La Paz has good diving services in town, including:

1. BAJA DIVING SERVICE — Located at Independencia 107 B, owned by the Aguilar Brothers. Has airfills, rentals, and guided tours. In the U.S., contact: Ph # 602-795-8777.

2. DEPORTIVA LA PAZ — located in the Malecon next to the Hotel La Perla. Has diving equipment sales and rentals, but no airfill services available.

3. TOTO'S DIVE — located at Guerrero and Revolution in Colonia Esterito, owned by Servio Nino de Rivera. Has airfills, rentals and guided tours.

A 3/16" or 1/4" wetsuit is recommended for the La Paz region during the late fall, winter and early spring months. From mid-June through mid-October, thanks to warmer water and air temperatures, a wetsuit is not generally required for warmth. However, it is advisable to wear a jacket top, protective clothing, or an 1/8" full wetsuit for protection from sharp rocks, sharp coral, stinging jellyfish and other irritants in the water.

Sportdiving in the La Paz region encompasses a wide variety of terrain, which includes diverse coastal areas and several large off-shore islands. Most of the charter boats radiating from La Paz head for the central Gulf region to the North between La Paz and Loreto, and particularly the islands in the San Jose Island region. There are few good beach diving sites near La Paz itself, as most of the better diving locations are accessible by boat only. Outstanding diving attractions accessible by local skiffs and small boats from the La Paz harbor include the wreck of the SALVATIERRA, the Islands of PARTIDA and ESPIRITU SANTO, the ISLOTES pinnacles and the underwater seamount called EL BAJO.

DIVE BOAT CHARTERS

Boat rentals and charters are easily secured in La Paz, through most of the tourist hotels, through the local dive shop, or through waterfront tourist enterprises. The following companies offer excellent charter boat diving tours for groups and individuals:

EXPEDICIONES BAJA
Owner: Ted Waltham
Mailing address: P.O. Box 120
                      La Paz, B.C.S. Mexico
Boat: THE BAJA EXPLORADOR

The Baja Explorador charter dive boat is 120′ long, with 10 staterooms (to accommodate 20 people), and semi-private heads and showers with hot and cold potable water. Features of the boat include: a well-equipped galley, large dining salon and bar, spacious deck room with individual storage lockers, 100V A.C. battery charging station, slide projector and 16mm projector, fishing and snorkeling gear, and a specimen collecting aquarium.

The boat is outfitted with an Ingersoll-Rand compressor to fill the 72 cu. ft. steel tanks on board. Tanks, weights and backpacks are provided, and diving is done directly from the boat or from the auxiliary skiffs and Boston Whalers. Night diving and shore excursions are available.

Large charter dive boats such as the DON JOSE enable divers to explore the more remote areas of the Sea of Cortez.

BAJA EXPEDITIONS
Owner: Tim Means
Mailing address: P.O. Box 3725
San Diego, CA 92103
Phone # (619) 297-0506
Boat: THE DON JOSE

The Don Jose charter dive boat is 80′ long, and outfitted with 5 staterooms (each accommodating 4 persons), all above deck, with heads and showers adjacent to the rooms. A large dining salon, a well-equipped galley, hot and cold potable water, ample deck room and an easy access swim step are some of the features of the boat. Added special equipment include darkroom facilities for black and white photo processing, fishing and snorkeling gear, slide projectors for evening slideshows, 100V A.C. battery recharging outlets, and a specimen collecting aquarium.

All diving is done from the boat itself or from one of 3 small skiffs with outboard motors. Twin Poseidon air compressors are used to fill the 80 cu. ft. aluminum tanks on board. Backpacks, weightbelts and tanks are provided. Night diving and shore excursions are available, weather permitting. The DON JOSE also charters whale-watching trips to Magdalene Bay during the winter months.

LA PAZ DIVING SERVICE
Owner: Richard Adcock
Mailing address: c/oBeverly International Travel
                94 Wilshire Blvd, Suite 832
                Beverly Hills, CA 90212
Phone # (213) 271-4116
Boat: THE MARISLA

The Marisla charter dive boat, formerly a buoy tender operating on the Sacramento River, is 120 feet long. It has eight staterooms, each with its own toilet and small sink. The boat offers a well-equipped galley, large dining room, spacious deck room, 100V A.C. battery charging station, fishing gear, and has several small chase boats for water-skiing, island exploring and diving.

Weights, weightbelts, tanks and backpacks are provided, and diving is done directly from the boat or from the small skiffs. Night diving is also available. The boat offers charters of from five to ten days' duration for groups of 16 or more. Cruises are available from April 15 through November 15, and custom itineraries can easily be arranged.

RIFFE ESCUELA DE BUCEO
Owners: John M. Riffe and family
Mailing address: c/o SEA SAFARIS
                3770 Highland Ave., Suite 102
                Manhattan Beach, CA 90266
Phone # (213) 546-2464; or 1-800-821-6670

Boat: THE RIO RITA

The Rio Rita charter dive boat is a 50' long charter boat. It does not have overnight accommodations, but offers good facilities for day diving excursions from La Paz for groups between 10 and 20 people. It has two compressors on board, as well as heads, a small galley, and fresh water showers. It also features a large swim step for diving from the boat, and also has a small skiff available for diving and shore excursions.

The Rio Rita offers group diving excursions from mid-March through mid-December. Groups are accommodated in a first-class hotel in La Paz nightly, and depart daily to dive local destinations near Espiritu Santo Island, including the Salvatierra shipwreck, the Islotes, and the Seamount. Normal charters include five days of diving, with breakfast and dinner in town, and lunch on the boat. Tanks and weights are provided, but divers should provide their own weight belts and backpacks.

DIVING LOCATIONS

Pichilingue Area

Pichilingue Bay, the site of the modern ferry terminal linking La Paz to Topolobampo and Mazatlan on mainland Mexico, is located 10 miles north of La Paz along the main road following the waterfront. The coves in and around the area were the center of much pirate activity in the past. Legends of marauding buccaneers and buried treasure were substantiated when a large chest of silver and gold coins was unearthed by workmen while excavating the new road to the area.

There are several tranquil coves, small islets and clean beaches around the Pichilingue area. Small trailerable and inflatable boats can be launched over the beach into the Bay along several beaches in the area. Due to its proximity to La Paz, and to its popularity with locals and tourists alike, marine life around the shoreline has been somewhat depleted. However, there are a few good scuba diving spots, and plenty of shallow areas for snorkeling.

PICHILINGUE BAY is easily reached by La Paz on a good paved road which terminates at the ferry terminal. A good dirt road continues a few hundred yards north to a public beach, which is an excellent point of departure for exploring the bay by small boats. Another dirt road also continues on to Ballandra Bay.

ISLA SAN JUAN NEPOMEZEINO is a long, low-lying islet which faces Pichilingue Bay. It would appear to be a good diving site, but depths around the island are shallow (30′ and less), consisting of sand, gravel and gradually sloping bottoms of small, barren rocks. Snorkeling

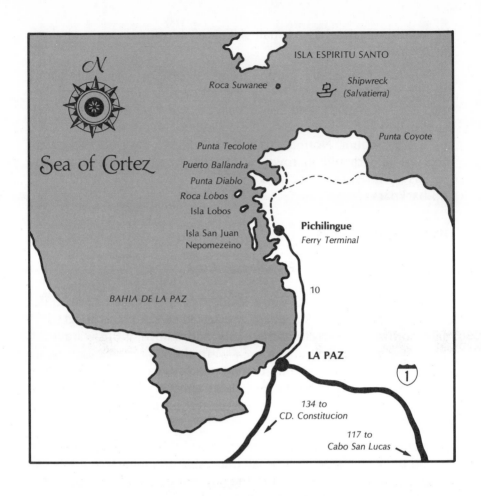

Pichilingue Area

reveals a few species of small tropical fish, including reef cornetfish and sergeant majors, but almost no invertebrate life.

ISLA LOBOS (also called La Gaviota) lies about 1/4 mile northwest of the Pichilingue public beach. It is easily recognized by its covering of white bird lime. Snorkeling is good along its shoreward side, with gently sloping depths to 40′ over a rocky terrain with scattered coral growths.

ROCA LOBOS is a small rock with a navigation light on top, lying about 1/4 mile northwest of ISLA LOBOS, and about 1/2 mile offshore. Snorkeling is good along its shoreward side, with depths of 10′ to 15′

along the shore. Scuba diving is good along its seaward side, where a rocky shore drops off rapidly to 60' and more over areas of alternating rocks and sand. Reef fish are fairly abundant, and occasional schools of pelagic fish frequent the area.

PUERTO BALLANDRA is a shallow protected bay known for its clear waters and fine, white beaches. The bay is a favorite clamming spot with locals, and a pleasant spot to spend a day in the sun swimming, snorkeling and beachcombing. Mangrove lagoons lie just back of the beach, however, and jejenes (biting gnats also called noseeums) can be fierce in the hotter months. A shallow reef protrudes about 5 feet above the water at low tide on the south side of the bay. This reef is an excellent snorkeling opportunity to glimpse a small and concentrated array of colorful sponges, coral and tropical fish.

PUNTA DIABLO lies at the southern point of Ballandra Bay. Small rocks along the shores drop to a sandy bottom floor to depths of 40', with several scattered caves and overhangs in the area. A good snorkeling reef, rich in invertebrate life, extends in a northerly direction off the point. It is visible above water at low tide.

SALVATIERRA SHIPWRECK lies in the San Lorenzo Channel between Espiritu Santo island and the Baja peninsula mainland. The Salvatierra is the name of the old La Paz-Topolobampo Ferry boat, which collided with a rock reef and sank off the southern end of Espiritu Santo island. When the ferry sank, there were no passengers aboard, only a cargo of trucks. The Salvatierra is one of the most popular dive sites near La Paz, but its popularity has thus far not disturbed the great numbers of fish and marine life on the wreck.

The ship has been salvaged, but the 300' hull is intact, and lies along the sandy ocean floor at a depth of 60'. Its mast peaks to within 20' of the surface. Outlying the ship in the sand are skeletons and frames of large trucks, with some of their giant wheels protruding from the sand. The shipwreck is thickly encrusted with marine life . . . sponges, sea fans, gorgonians, scallops, oysters, and other colorful invertebrate life. Schools of silvery bait fish and greybar grunt swarm over the wreck, and colorful angelfish, surgeonfish, sergeant majors, pufferfish, snapper, Mexican barracuda and grouper also frequent the hull.

The wreck of the Salvatierra ferry boat is one of the most popular dive sites near La Paz.

The Salvatierra is located in the narrow San Lorenzo Channel approximately 1-1/2 miles off the south end of ISLA ESPIRITU SANTO. Strong currents can arise quickly through the channel. Currents and surface wind chop can disturb visibility considerably. It is best to dive the wreck when currents are minimal. The shipwreck is best located through local guides, or with a fathometer. The dark hull can also be seen from the surface on a calm day when water visibility is good.

This is one of the most outstanding fish photography sites in the area. During the early summer months, the breeding behavior of the Panamic sergeant major fish can be observed on the shipwreck. The males clean small areas on the hull by rubbing their bellies over the surface, in order to clear away the algae for a nest site. The males assume a deep metallic blue color to attract females to the nest to deposit their eggs. They guard their nests, which appear as round purple-colored patches, until the eggs hatch later in the summer.

Espiritu Santo and Partida Islands

Eighteen miles north of the city of La Paz just outside the La Paz Harbor lie the islands of Espiritu Santo and Partida. Their protected coves, fine beaches, and clear waters are frequented seasonally by sailors, fishermen and divers. Sportdiving opportunities around the islands are exciting and diverse, and are usually limited only by the prevailing wind conditions.

The northernmost island of Partida is barely separated from Espiritu Santo by a small tidal passage, which appears as a long, narrow indentation between the two islands. From a distance, the two islands appear as one. Their combined length totals 12 miles. The closest point to the Baja mainland is a distance of 5 miles, directly off the southern end.

THE WESTERN SHORELINE is the favored side of the islands with boaters, because of the numerous protected coves and beaches that carve the coastline in deep indentations. The white sands and emerald waters of the coves are reminiscent of Caribbean islands, but the rocky undersea terrain remains consistent with that found elsewhere around La Paz. Most of the coves along the islands are fairly shallow, but rocky ledges bordering their entrances frequently drop to depths of 50' to 60'. Several good diving reefs lie along the western side of the islands.

SAN GABRIEL BAY is the first large cove on Espiritu Santo Island north of the San Lorenzo Channel. At the northwestern entrance to SAN GABRIEL BAY lies a series of natural grottos carved from the cliffs by wind and water. Immediately west of these grottos just off the point lies a good snorkeling and shallow diving reef. Rocky ledges and boulders are clustered between sandy channels at depths averaging 40' and less. This point is well protected from northerly winds.

ISLA BALLENA (WHALE ISLAND) is a small rocky island just south of Candelero Cove about 1/2 mile off the western side of Espiritu Santo Island. Two smaller islets called EL GALLO and LA GALLINA (meaning The Rooster and the Hen) lie about 1-1/2 miles southeastward of this small island. The two smaller islets are surrounded by predominantly shoal and barren rock and sandy terrain, while the larger island of BALLENA has deeper rocky shores with good diving locations in its surrounding waters.

The west and northwest sides of ISLA BALLENA are good diving sites, with rocky shorelines sloping underwater to depths ranging from 30' to over 100'. A rocky reef extends from shore off the western end of the island, dropping gradually to depths of 100' close around the island. Schools of fish frequent the deeper areas, with sporadic growths of corals growing along the submerged rocky boulders. Small tropical fish and moray eels are found in shallower areas. This small island affords an alternate dive site when southerly winds disturb other sites in the area.

CALETA PARTIDA (Partida Cove) is the narrow indentation between Espiritu Santo and Partida, that ends in a low spit of sand and rock comprising the connecting point of land between the two islands. A tidal channel (3 to 5 feet deep at high tide) in the sand spit affords small boats access through the channel. A rocky reef about 1/4 mile long on the northern side of the entrance to Partida Cove protrudes in a southwestern direction off the point. It is covered by water at high tide, and resembles a "backbone" of large boulders. Depths along the reef range from 40' to 60', terminating in large sandy areas.

ENSENADA GRANDE is the northernmost inlet located on the western side of ISLA PARTIDA, offering a good sheltered anchorage from most prevailing winds. Good diving locations are found around a small "backbone-like" ridge of rocks extending off the northern point of Ensenada Grande, running in a southwestern direction. Shallow depths prevail on its south side, dropping to 35' and 40'. The northwestern face of the reef extends to deeper waters, with depths averaging 60'. This reef is characterized by its unusual clusters of gigantic rock boulders, which lie along a sandy bottom. The reef is not extremely colorful, but large caves and crevices in the rocks house some tropical reef fish. Schools of garden eels and cabrilla can be seen along the sandy areas.

THE EASTERN SHORELINE of Partida and Espiritu Santo Islands is characterized by steep, rocky cliffs broken by small stretches of sand and gravel beaches. The waters on this side of the islands are not as protected from prevailing winds as they are along the western shore of the islands, and there are few good boat anchorages along this shoreline. The eastern shoreline is open to strong northwesterlies which generally occur between November and May, and is also open to the summer southerly wind conditions as well. This coast is seldom frequented by diving charters, due to the inadequate wind protection, but rocky points along the shoreline generally drop off sharply and are abundant with marine life.

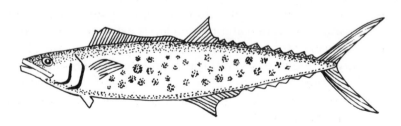

SIERRA MACKEREL
Scomberomorus sierra

The unusual rock formations at Los Islotes pinnacles provide a dramatic backdrop to diving in the area.

EL BAJITO (The Shallow Reef) is the name given a large, SUBMERGED REEF area located about 1/2 mile southwest of the west end of LOS ISLOTES. The reef peaks within 20′ of the surface, and drops to depths of 80′ and 90′ along its outer edges where the rocks meet the sand. The terrain and marine life is extremely interesting and diverse. The top of the reef is characterized by long, narrow alleyways that are large enough to swim through and that are lined with orange TUBASTREA coral. Moray eels are extremely abundant on the reef and varieties of colorful tropical fish present outstanding fish photography opportunities on the reef.

Along deeper areas of the reef, from 60′ to 90′, there are prolific gardens of colorful sea fans and gorgonian corals growing on large and medium sized boulders. Schooling fish, grouper and cabrilla appear in the deeper and cooler waters. Strong currents and lack of wind protection present hazards to diving this reef, but on a calm day with minimal currents this is an excellent diving site. The reef can usually be spotted from the surface on a calm day, with the top of the reef comprised of broad expanses of smooth, flat rocks.

LOS ISLOTES (The Islets) is one of the most popular diving sites in the area, and those who return again and again to dive these tiny islets seldom tire of the experience. LOS ISLOTES is located across an 800-foot wide channel separating them from the north point of PARTIDA ISLAND. This tiny group of isolated rocks whitened by bird lime is characterized by steep, vertical walls that house nests for a variety of birds in the area, including frigates, gulls and the brown boobies. A high, narrow crevice pierces through the easternmost rock and is just wide enough for a small boat to navigate through on a calm day. Diving is excellent and varied around the entire circumference of its rocky shoreline.

LOS ISLOTES is inhabited by a friendly colony of sea lions who occupy a large cove in the center of the south side of the islands. These sea lions seem to enjoy swimming and playing right alongside divers in the area. Diving with and photographing this friendly group of sea lions is one of the biggest attractions at this dive site. Sea lions have their young in the early summer months.

Gently sloping rocks dominate the submarine terrain within the cove, with depths of 10' to 60', and numerous tropical fish species. From mid-April throughout the summer, the Cortez Damselfish deposit their eggs in the rocky crevices lining the cove (as do the sergeant major fish), vigorously guarding their territories. At the base of the rocks in 60' to 80' of water, the tiny blue-spotted jawfish makes its home in the sand. The backside, or northern shore of ISLOTES, exhibits large rocks and boulders sloping downward to depths of 80' to 90', ending in sandy areas. The rocky reefs around the northwest and western sides are generally lacking in invertebrate life, but house some tropical fish species.

The most colorful areas are located along the northeast and eastern shores of LOS ISLOTES, where depths drop to over 100' and large boulders and pinnacles covered with colorful sea fans and gorgonians cluster around sandy areas. Schools of cabrilla, sharks, pelagic jacks, and giant manta rays cruise along the sand at the edge of the rocks, and colorful angelfish, surgeonfish, parrotfish, snappers and goatfish are also abundant. Currents in the area are strongest around this point, and the point is also open to surge from adverse wind conditions.

An interesting way to explore this point is to enter the large vertical crevice that cuts through the rock, where shallow depths (30' and less) prevail. Then continue diving around the point to the east, exploring the deeper areas off the eastern side (where rocky slopes drop to 80' to 90', ending in sand). Schooling fish and large game fish can be seen at the base of these rocks. Then continue around the point back to the entrance of the cave again in the shallows, or continue on to the sea lion rookery in the shallow cove along the south shore of Los Islotes.

EL BAJO (THE SEAMOUNT) is a submerged group of three large rocky pinnacles rising abruptly from deep waters and running in a north-south direction. These pinnacles lie approximately 10 miles northeast of Los Islotes. The northernmost pinnacle rises to within 80' of the surface; the middle pinnacle rises to within 50'; and the southern pinnacle peaks within 60' of the surface. Depths around the pinnacles drop off quickly to 125', with smaller pinnacles situated around their bases. The bottom then gradually slopes deeper, with depths reaching over 1,800 feet within 1/2 mile of the seamounts.

The center pinnacle (the shallowest one) is the largest and most frequently dived pinnacle in the area. Its south end is comprised of a steep-walled vertical cliff that drops off abruptly from 50' to 110', its base situated along a large, sandy channel often frequented by hammerhead sharks and large grouper. The top of the large peak is comprised of a series of narrow rocky alleyways with sandy channels that are large enough to swim through (depths: 60' to 65'). Large moray eels inhabit the narrow fissures in the rocky surfaces, and schools of tropical fish abound. Small sea fans and gorgonians cover the top portion of the seamount, while larger and more colorful ones begin at depths of 80' to 90'. There are several small caves at the 100' base of the seamount. The seamount is primarily known for its abundance of pelagic fish that visit the area, including sharks (hammerhead, dusky, black tip, silver tip, tiger), corvina, jacks, marlin, dorado, manta rays and an occasional whale shark.

Diving on the Seamount necessitates very careful use of the decompression tables, which requires an accurate depth and pressure gauge. With the shallowest peak rising to within 50' of the surface, it is very easy to descend deeper than planned and to lose track of depths. With open ocean diving conditions prevailing, this is no place for novice divers.

An unusual encounter with a giant manta ray at the Seamount. (photo: Howard Hall)

This group of underwater SEAMOUNTS is one of the most famous dive sites in the entire Sea of Cortez. Its renown derives from the unusual behavior of the marine life in the area. Giant manta rays that appear around the Seamounts during the late summer and early fall months often exhibit unusually friendly behavior, actually allowing divers to ride upon their backs and sometimes initiating this contact over and over again. Manta rays (Manta Hamiltoni) are plankton eaters, and do not possess any type of stinging barbs or poisoned spines. They can reach more than 3,000 pounds and 25 feet across, and are extremely strong and swift.

The unusual behavior of these manta rays has been observed and documented by scuba divers and scientists alike over a period of several years, and there is no doubt that it is the manta ray who ultimately decides if he is in the mood for a hitchhiking scuba diver.

And, once the diver is on his back, the manta ray can quite easily dislodge the diver by a quick flip of his wings and an abrupt and swift departure into the depths. Any diver who has had the rare opportunity of sharing an encounter with one of these giant manta rays should feel truly privileged. For most, it is like realizing a childhood fantasy of flying through the air on the back of some mythical winged creature.

During these same months, large schools of scalloped hammerhead sharks appear around the Seamount. The scalloped hammerhead (Sphyrna lewini) is a potentially dangerous shark species, and can reach a length up to 12 feet. However, during this type of schooling behavior these sharks rarely exhibit any type of aggressive behavior, and even seem to shy away from divers. What makes their behavior even more unusual is that normally, sharks don't school together.

Marine scientists have been studying the schooling behavior of the scalloped hammerheads in the Sea of Cortez for a number of years now. While it is suspected that their schooling behavior may be related to mating, they have thus far found very little proof and are still unable to draw any definitive conclusions as to why scalloped hammerhead sharks school together in such large numbers.

The scalloped hammerhead schools in large numbers around the Seamount, and often approaches within close distance of divers. (photo: Howard Hall).

To Punta Pescadero

The coastline southward of La Paz, from the San Lorenzo Channel to Punta Pescadero, encompasses a 50-mile long stretch of coastline with good diving locations along several of its prominent rocky bluffs. The southernmost island in the Sea of Cortez, CERRALVO ISLAND, is also located opposite this coastline, and offers several excellent diving sites around its rocky shoreline and surrounding waters.

PUNTA COYOTE TO BAHIA VENTANA comprises a bold and rocky coastline with intervening gravel and sand beaches lining several small coves. There are several ranching settlements, fishing villages, private homes, sportfishing resorts and small airstrips along the coast that connect with La Paz by generally rough roads that are often impassable during the rainy season. Diving along this shore is limited, however, by the lack of good access roads as well as lack of wind protection and comfortable anchorages along much of the shoreline. The best diving areas are typically located around groups of detached rocks that off-lie bold promontories of land projecting from shore along the coast. Otherwise, much of the coastal terrain reveals generally shallow depths with barren rock and cobblestone areas or shallow sandy areas.

A good, partially paved and gravelled road located three miles south of La Paz turns left for 30 miles into the agricultural region of LOS PLANES. This dirt road continues past Los Planes for a distance of 12 miles and then branches off into smaller roads which lead into BAHIA VENTANA, CUEVA DE LEON and MUERTOS BAY. Limited grocery supplies are available at Los Planes, and presently the only tourist facilities in the region comprise a large, private fly-in resort hotel called "Las Arenas," stretching across the beachfront at Cueva de Leon. There are several excellent diving locations along this relatively short stretch of coastline.

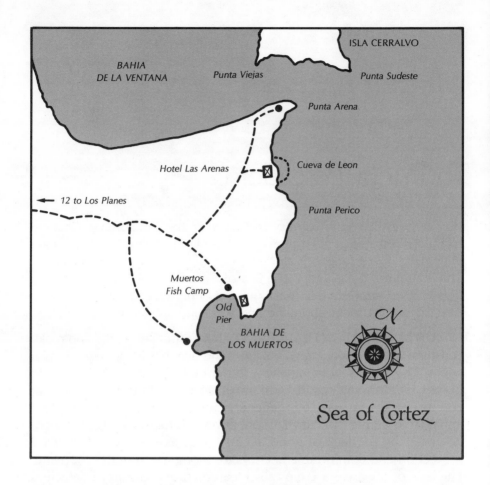

Ventana Bay to Muertos Bay

BAHIA VENTANA (Window Bay) is a large, open expanse of bay sheltered from the east by Cerralvo Island. Its southernmost point, PUNTA ARENA DE LA VENTANA (The Sandy Point of Window Bay), is the closest point of land to Cerralvo Island which is located 5 miles across the channel. A road leads into the southeastern shore of BAHIA VENTANA, where local fishermen launch their small skiffs and depart to fish the surrounding waters.

CUEVA DE LEON (Sea Lion's Cave). The large, sweeping expanse of beach that fronts VENTANA BAY continues south around PUNTA ARENA to the sculptured rock formations along the shores of Cueva de Leon, where the palm-lined swimming pool of a private fly-in resort hotel faces the sea.

An underwater wall drops just off the beach in front of the resort and follows the configuration of the shoreline southward. The wall drops almost vertically to a sandy bottom in depths of 30' to 40'. Corals, sea fans and sponges line the rock crevices along the wall, and schools of parrotfish, yellowtail, surgeonfish and angelfish are common in the area. Just out from the submarine cliff lie a series of large, isolated submerged boulders which are etched with sculptured grottos and crevices lined with orange TUBASTREA corals and small sea fans. There is no beach access to this dive site except through the hotel (which is generally not open to the public); so it is best to visit the area by small boats launched over the beach north at VENTANA BAY.

PUNTA PERICO (Parrot Point . . . possibly named after the large schools of parrotfish in the area, which are called "Pez Perico" in Spanish; or may also derive its name from the aboriginal "Pericue" Indians that once inhabited the region.) It is a prominent rocky bluff located between CUEVA DE LEON and MUERTOS BAY. It lies about 2½ miles north of Muertos Bay. The coastline south of PERICO POINT is steep with underwater vertical drop-offs close to shore. Depths around the point drop to 60' to 90', exhibiting a sandy bottom interspersed with large rocks. Cold currents arising from the submarine trench along the coast foster generally good visibilities, and the reefs are rich in fish and invertebrate life.

The north end of PUNTA PERICO is an excellent diving location. Gigantic boulders with steep submarine faces plunge dramatically to depths of 80', in a series of giant steps descending downward. Large schools of fish sweep in around the point, and scallops and murex shells are common on the rocks.

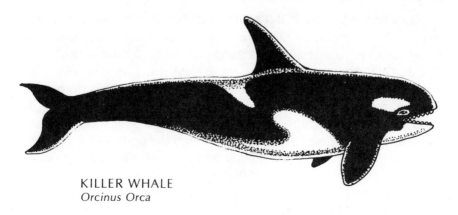

KILLER WHALE
Orcinus Orca

LOS MUERTOS BAY. As Punta Perico approaches Los Muertos Bay, the depths near shore become shallower and a series of rocky outcroppings form finger-like reefs along sandy areas. With depths of 10' or less close to shore, snorkeling is good around these reefs. A rocky terrain interspersed with sandy areas slopes very gradually from the shoreline to depths of only 50' about ¼ mile offshore.

The road from Los Planes branches southward into Muertos Bay for approximately 1 mile after the VENTANA BAY turnoff, and ends at a small fishing settlement near the old pier. Camping is possible back of the beach to the south of the fishing camp, and car-top and inflatable boats can be launched into the bay over the beach. This bay is a popular sailboat anchorage, with a beautiful sweeping expanse of beach along the cove.

Inside Muertos Bay itself, shallow depths predominate (30' and less), along a predominantly sandy sea floor. An old pier, which was built by a silver mining company in 1925, lies at the north end of the bay. Broken remnants of the mining operation may be seen underwater scattered around the bay (ore carts, rails, anchors, etc.). There are several species of reef fish in the area, but very little invertebrate life.

A small cove at the south end of the bay is accessible by a rough dirt road best suited for high clearance vehicles. This road branches south off the road from Los Planes approximately 1 mile before reaching the VENTANA BAY turnoff. It then continues over rough terrain for a distance of 5 miles. The road is often used by local fishermen. A lovely beach fronts the cove, and shallow reefs around the cove are good snorkeling areas.

MUERTOS BAY TO PUNTA PESCADERO The coastline south of Muertos Bay is characterized by a series of low-lying rocky points and gravel beaches, continuing a distance of about 22 miles to PUNTA PESCADERO (the northern limit of BAHIA DE LAS PALMAS). The underwater terrain along this stretch of rocky coastline is dominated by medium-sized rocks and boulders, sloping to gradual depths of 40' to 50' close inshore scattered along sandy areas. Both snorkeling and diving are good along this shoreline, though the underwater terrain is generally barren-looking and fine silt which covers the rocks can easily disturb visibility. Large game fish and schools of tropical reef fish inhabit the reefs, in addition to typical invertebrate life, moray eels, and diverse shell life (rock scallops and murex).

Picturesque Muertos Bay is a popular camping and diving site south of La Paz.

Isla Cerralvo

The southernmost island in the Sea of Cortez, Cerralvo Island, is for the most part barren and uninhabited. It is 16 miles long and 4 miles wide. At the time of its discovery by Spanish explorers, the island was inhabited by a primitive tribe of Indians called the Pericues. Extensive pearl oyster beds were discovered along its western shore, and the island became one of the main sources of Baja pearls during the pearling era.

Cerralvo Island is usually accessed by boat from La Paz, or from small skiffs across the channel on the mainland near BAHIA VENTANA or from MUERTOS BAY. A distance of 5 miles separates the island from its closest point to the mainland, which is PUNTA ARENA DE LA VENTANA. The island contains several sheltered coves, and two or three anchorages lie abreast its shoreward side. Landings may be made on beaches near the southern end of the island, or near the mouth of small "arroyos" which open along its otherwise steep and imposing coastline.

PIEDRAS GORDAS is located along the southwestern end of Cerralvo Island between Punto Viejos and Punta Sudeste. It is a bold rocky point with a good landing beach and small anchorage along its northwest end. A wide expanse of shallow rocky reefs extends about ¼ mile from the shoreline in a series of finger-like formations. Depths range from 10′ around the reefs awash close inshore to 40′ to 50′ along their outer edges where they end in sandy areas several hundred yards from shore. Scattered coral formations and sea fans frame numerous ledges and overhangs, and a good abundance of tropical fish frequent the reefs, including schools of yellowtail surgeonfish and brightly colored parrotfish. This is also a good nightdiving location, due to the relatively shallow depths and an abundance of marine life.

PUNTA SUDESTE is a steep rocky bluff at the southeastern side of the island. It is an excellent diving location in calm weather when currents are minimal. Surge and currents in the area present potential hazards for diving around this point. Large boulders in cathedral-like formations lie isolated along sandy areas in depths that drop to 60′ close around the point. Their steep rocky faces are lined with thick growths of indigo and red sea fans and gorgonian corals. Tropical reef fish hover around the rocks, and schools of game fish frequently sweep in around the point.

THE EASTERN SIDE of the island is dominated by rocky bluffs which drop almost vertically into the water. Sharp descents continue underwater, reaching depths of 600′ several hundred yards offshore. The entire eastern shore of the island affords no anchorages or landing beaches, except for occasional steep arroyos that end in small gravel beaches. A deep submarine trench closely approaches this side of the island, and pelagic game fish and large reef fish frequent the rocky areas along the edge of the trench.

THE NORTHERN TIP of Cerralvo Island presents a series of protruding jagged rocks which break away from the coast to form a submerged reef that continues northward for nearly half a mile. Depths average 60′ to 70′ along the reef. Sea lions inhabit the outermost rocks, and the reefs are fed by cold-water currents from a deep submarine trench nearby, insuring an abundance of marine life. This is a spectacular diving site, but the area lacks protection from prevailing wind conditions and strong currents can arise quickly around the point.

The sharp spines on the Crown-of-Thorns starfish can cause a very painful wound.

Fern-like hydroids, which grow in feathery clumps along rocky reefs, can produce stinging skin irritations.

ISLOTE DE LA REINA (also called SEAL ROCK) is an isolated group of detached rocks lying about four miles directly off the northwestern end of the island. It comprises a small rock, about 100 feet long and 50 feet wide, protruding about 15 feet above the water with a navigation light atop a metal tower on the rock. Several other submerged rocks lie nearby, either awash at low tide or with very shallow depths over them. Depths drop off sharply around the rocks, to 50' and 60', with depths of 150' found less than ¼ mile from the rock.

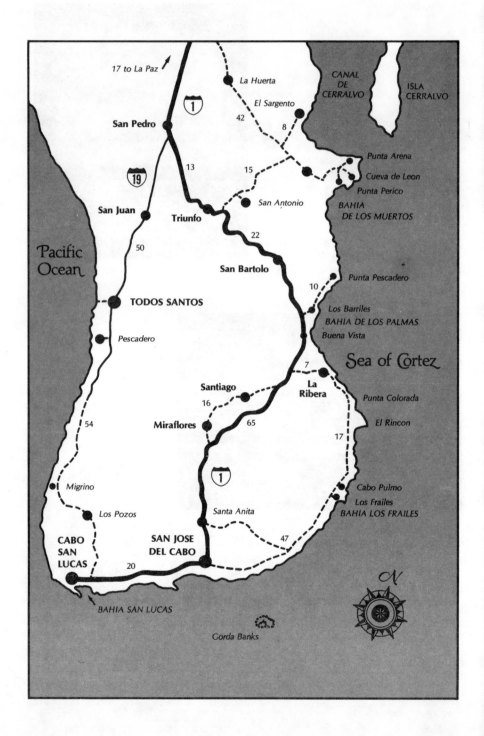

17 to La Paz

La Huerta

CANAL
DE
CERRALVO

ISLA
CERRALVO

El Sargento

42

8

San Pedro

13

15

Punta Arena

Cueva de Leon

Punta Perico

BAHIA
DE LOS MUERTOS

San Juan

Triunfo

San Antonio

22

Pacific
Ocean

50

San Bartolo

10

Punta Pescadero

TODOS SANTOS

Los Barriles
BAHIA DE LOS PALMAS
Buena Vista

Pescadero

Sea of Cortez

7

Santiago

La
Ribera

Punta Colorada

16

El Rincon

Miraflores

65

17

54

1

Migrino

Cabo Pulmo

Los Pozos

Santa Anita

Los Frailes
BAHIA LOS FRAILES

CABO
SAN
LUCAS

SAN JOSE
DEL CABO

47

20

N

BAHIA SAN LUCAS

Gorda Banks

184

The Cape Region

The "Cape Region" (Los Cabos) comprises the southernmost portion of the Baja Peninsula, from Punta Pescadero south to Cabo San Lucas. Baja's transpeninsular Highway 1 continues south from La Paz for a distance of 130 miles before abruptly terminating at the charming seaside resort of Cabo San Lucas. Here the famous "land's end" granite archway plunges into the sea, marking the end of the 800-mile long Baja California peninsula, and separating the waters of the Cortez from the Pacific Ocean. The protected waters of the Cabo San Lucas Bay were once a favorite hiding place for pirates and buccaneers, who would lie in wait behind the "land's end" pinnacles to plunder the treasure-laden Spanish galleons enroute from the Philippines. Today, cruising yachts, sleek sailboats and tourist-laden cruise ships drop anchor, seeking a different type of treasure along its peaceful shores.

The Cape Region is a region of startling beauty and contrasts. Miles of white sand beaches stretch invitingly along the coastline, their vast expanses interrupted by spectacular granite rock formations fashioned from aeons of time and weather. Ultra-modern resorts line the shores like small oases, with their jeweled swimming pools, brightly-colored tile and lush tropical palms set in stark contrast to the arid Mexican desert behind them. Luxury yachts and oceanliners, hotels and condominiums, and restaurants and discoteques all compete for space in this tropical paradise setting. The Cape Region enjoys the mildest weather in the Sea of Cortez. Its remarkable natural beauty enchants and intrigues all who visit its shores.

The waters of the southern Cape Region have long been popular with sportfishermen. They also hold a remarkable variety of sportdiving attractions, including some of the most abundant and colorful varieties of tropical marine life found in the entire Sea of

The view of San Lucas Bay, site of the underwater sand falls, from one of the picturesque hotels in Cabo San Lucas.

Cortez. The largest living coral reef in the Sea of Cortez is located in this region, as are the famous underwater "sand falls" which cascade down the sides of steep submarine canyons. This region usually boasts the clearest and warmest waters in the Cortez, and sportdiving is possible year round, limited only by occasionally strong winds.

TOURIST FACILITIES

The Cape Region of Baja California is famous for some of the most attractive and luxurious seaside resorts in all of Baja California. Each resort offers its own unique charm and beauty. Some are magnificently perched on rocky cliffs overlooking the ocean, while others sprawl sumptuously across sandy coves reaching down to the water's edge.

The two major centers of tourism in the area are the small towns of Cabo San Lucas at the tip of the peninsula, and San Jose del Cabo, 22 miles north of Cabo San Lucas. These two towns are often referred to as "LOS CABOS," meaning the Capes. A large, international jet airport is located near San Jose del Cabo, and services all of the hotels in the area. An excellent RV and trailer park with modern facilities is located in San Jose del Cabo, just south of the Presidente Hotel, and camping is also possible along some of the beaches in the area.

Cabo San Lucas is an international port of entry into Mexico, and all visiting yachts are required to register with the Office of the Port Captain. A large ferry terminal is located in the harbor at Cabo San Lucas, offering trans-ocean ferry service for cars and passengers to and from PUERTO VALLARTA on the Mexican mainland. Both towns offer a good selection of grocery supplies, as well as international communications, modern medical facilities and connecting bus services to other parts of the Baja peninsula.

BOAT LAUNCHING

A good paved boat launching ramp is located in the marina at Cabo San Lucas. Trailered boats of any size can be launched here. Car-top and small-to-medium sized trailered boats may be launched from several beaches along the coast, but over-the-beach launching with larger boats requires 4-wheel drive vehicles.

DIVING

There is presently no professional dive shop located in the Cape Region, but there are several diving concessions where airfills can be obtained, equipment can be rented and a dive guide and boat can be hired. However, it is best to inquire about airfills, rentals and dive trips at least one day prior to planning your dive, so that you can reserve the necessary equipment and can insure that airfills are available. Airfills, equipment rentals, and diving guides may be arranged through the following agencies:

1. **Paraiso Diving Services**—located at Medano Beach, Cabo San Lucas Bay, next to the Las Palmas Restaurant. This diving service is usually open from 8 to 5, and has a good compressor on their premises. Paraiso Diving service offers equipment rentals, scuba instruction from a PADI instructor, airfills, and boat and diving guide services. The price for a boat and guide usually begins at $25.00 per person.

2. **The Hotel Hacienda**—located right on the beach facing the San Lucas Bay. The Hotel Hacienda has a sports concession stand facing the beach, and has a compressor on the premises. They offer equipment rentals, airfills and guides and skiffs are available for hire. Larger sportfishing boats can also be chartered through the Hotel for diving (prices start at $150.00/day with crew).

3. **Amigos del Mar**—a private diving service operated by Jose Luis Sanchez, offering scuba and snorkeling tours with bilingual certified dive masters. This service can be presently contacted through the Solmar or Finisterra Hotels, but may expand into a full service dive shop in the future.

4. **Hotel Punta Pescadero**—is located in the northern portion of the Cape Region, at the north end of the Bahia Las Palmas just north of Cabo Pulmo. It is located 8 miles north of Los Barriles, branching off the main highway. A Poseidon compressor services diver's airfill needs at the hotel. Snorkeling and scuba equipment is available for rent, and diving trips can also be arranged.

From November through May a 1/8" or 3/16" wetsuit is recommended for warmth and protection. During the summer months, some type of protective clothing (or thin wetsuit) should be worn for protection from sharp coral and rocks, and stinging marine life.

DEEP DIVING: It should be re-emphasized that there are no recompression chamber facilities readily available in Baja California. There are several diving locations in the Cape Region where it is possible to reach depths over 100' very quickly (as in the submarine canyon at Cabo San Lucas), so extreme caution concerning depths should be exercised. Decompression tables should be used to plan deep or multiple dives and a reliable depth gauge is a must.

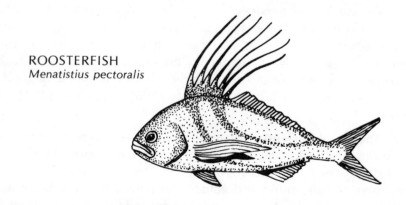

ROOSTERFISH
Menatistius pectoralis

DIVING LOCATIONS

Punta Pescadero to Cabo Pulmo

The coastline between Punta Pescadero and Cabo Pulmo is dominated by a large open bay called BAHIA DE LAS PALMAS. This bay is noted for its remarkable abundance of seasonal game fish, and several modern fishing resorts offering excellent accommodations and facilities are located along the shores of the region. A deep submarine trench closely parallels this coastline, and cold-water upwellings from the canyon's depths provide nutrients for a rich abundance of marine life in the area. Large schools of fish feed close inshore in the protected edges of the submarine trench. Marlin, sailfish, dolphinfish, tuna, yellowtail, wahoo, roosterfish, snapper, sierra mackerel, and bonito crowd the shores of the region seasonally, providing excellent fishing grounds for the sportfishing resorts that dominate this coastline.

The beautiful fishing resort of HOTEL PUNTA PESCADERO is the only hotel in the region that has its own air compressor for sportdivers, and caters to sportdivers as well as fishermen. it is located 8 miles north of Los Barriles, and lies 15 miles south of MUERTOS BAY. The mailing address of the hotel is: HOTEL PUNTA PESCADERO, BOX 1044, Los Altos, CA 94022. Phone (415) 948-5505). Other tourist resorts along the coastline primarily cater to sportfishermen, although some will arrange diving tours for their customers upon request, traveling to La Paz to obtain tanks and airfills.

PUNTA PESCADERO The hotel is situated on a rocky bluff just south of PUNTA PESCADERO, the bold rocky point of land that comprises the northern limit of BAHIA DE LAS PALMAS. Detached rocks lie close off the point in front of the hotel, as well as close around PESCADERO POINT situated several hundred yards north. Off both of these points lie good snorkeling and shallow diving locations, with underwater terrain comprised of rocky areas scattered sporadically along a sandy ocean floor. Shallow depths of 30' and less prevail, with sporadic growths of colorful sea fans and hard stony corals attached to the rocks. Moray eels, lobster, and tropical reef fish inhabit the reefs, and schools of pompano and jacks often appear to feed along the edges of the reefs, where schools of garden eels make their homes in sandy areas.

Las Palmas Bay is known for its great numbers of large, pelagic game fish.

HOTEL PUNTA PESCADERO offers airfills from a Poseidon compressor, as well as limited equipment rental which includes tanks, backpack, weights and snorkeling gear. Sportfishing boats and small skiffs can be chartered from the hotel, and diving tours with local guides can be arranged.

PUNTA COLORADO is the large promontory of land about 16 miles southeast of Punta Pescadero that forms the southern limit of BAHIA DE LAS PALMAS. A large resort hotel, HOTEL PUNTA COLORADO, is situated along a wide sandy beach just southward of the point. The hotel does not presently have diving facilities on its premises, but can make arrangements for diving trips for its customers by prior reservations. Rocky patches of reefs and detached rocks lie close around the hotel for snorkeling and shallow diving, and other shoal reef areas located sporadically along the coast can be reached by boat from the hotel. The coastline from Punta Colorado south to Cabo Pulmo is comprised primarily of long stretches of sand beaches.

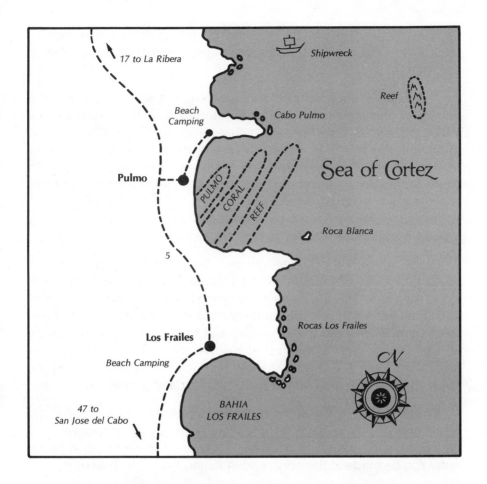

Cabo Pulmo and Los Frailes

The coastal region of CABO PULMO AND LOS FRAILES is accessible by a dirt road which leaves Highway 1 about 75 miles south of La Paz (and eight miles south of the Rancho Buena Vista turnoff). After leaving the main highway heading south, the dirt road turns east for 8 miles into the small town of LA RIBERA, where limited grocery supplies and a PEMEX gasoline station can be found. The road then continues south for 28 miles to CABO PULMO. Los Frailes Bay is located 2 miles farther south of Cabo Pulmo along the same dirt road. The dirt road into CABO PULMO is passable with standard cars to Los Frailes. After Los Frailes, this road extends south along the coast for 47 miles to San Jose del Cabo, but the road is presently recommended for 4-wheel drive vehicles. Improvements are planned on the road, but it is best to inquire with locals as to the status of improvements on this stretch of the road.

This region, once remote and isolated, is beginning to feel the impact of the expanding tourist development in the Cape Region. When the road between Los Frailes and San Jose del Cabo is improved, this coastline is likely to sprout many more tourist facilities than it now has. Presently, there are nearby resort hotels located north of the Pulmo area, but otherwise, tourist facilities along this stretch of the coast are minimal. Most who visit the region are generally self-contained. Camping is available along beaches in the area, and there is a small restaurant at the settlement back of Pulmo Bay.

Divers who bring portable air compressors or their own supply of scuba tanks into this region will be able to dive some beautiful reefs along the coast. This area is ideal for diving from small inflatable boats, and small skiffs can also be rented from local fishermen in the area. Small to medium-sized trailered boats can be launched over the beach at Los Frailes, but a 4-wheel drive vehicle is recommended for launching. There are several shallow reefs and rocky points along the coast that are also well suited for snorkeling and free diving.

CABO PULMO is the name of the large promontory located at the north end of Pulmo Bay. Shallow water extends off this cape in all directions, with numerous detached rocks around the point. A beach entry can be made at the north end of Pulmo Beach, with a short swim (150') to arrive at the point for snorkeling or diving. The rocky shoreline along the south side of the point drops to depths of 20' or less, with lobster, moray eels, small tropical fish, schooling sierra mackerel and occasional schools of jacks and roosterfish frequenting the point.

The underwater terrain around the point itself is characterized by large rocks and boulders separated by sandy channels. Depths range from 40' to 60' close around the point. A large, submerged pinnacle is located about 20 yards east of the point, rising to within 15' of the surface. The shore side of this pinnacle drops to a depth of 30' along a rocky bottom. Its seaward side plummets steeply to 60' before sloping gradually deeper. Large game fish sweep in around the point, and the pinnacle is covered with sporadic hard coral growths, sea fans, and other invertebrate life.

The unique stony coral heads at Cabo Pulmo house numerous species of semi-tropical fish, such as this exquisite long-nose butterflyfish.

CABO PULMO CORAL REEF is the most famous underwater attraction in the area, and is one of the most unique marine phenomena in the Sea of Cortez. The CABO PULMO CORAL REEFS are the only coral reefs in the Sea of Cortez, as well as on the entire west coast of North America. These unique coral reefs owe their existence to the water temperatures in the CABO PULMO BAY, which stay a pleasant 70° F. year-round. (Reef-building corals can only survive in tropical waters where the temperature never falls below 70° F.) The protected and shallow waters inside the PULMO BAY are not exposed to the effects of the cold-water upwellings and currents common throughout the Sea of Cortez, which mix with warmer surface waters and cause seasonal water temperature fluctuations. There are no coral reef formations farther north in the Gulf for precisely this reason: surface water temperatures fluctuate from warm in summer to very cool in winter, prohibiting the growths of reef-building corals.

The coral reefs in Pulmo Bay consist of a series of eight long bars of extruded igneous rock, upon which coral and other marine flora and fauna grow. All eight of these bars extend out from the beach and are easily visible, resembling rocky dikes that project from the sand and continue into the sea.

Common marine life around the coral reefs includes: White-banded angelfish, moray eels, lobster, pufferfish, yellowtail, surgeonfish, porkfish, butterflyfish, parrotfish, moorish idol, hawkfish, and blennies. Along the deeper reefs, schools of barred grunts and schooling game fish and large grouper appear, as well as a greater abundance of gorgonians and sea fans. The yellow gorgonian (Eunicia sp.) is the largest and most dominant of these corals. Tubastrea corals and red sea fans are also abundant, and the spectacular spiny red sea star (Oreaster occidentalis) appears around rock groupings in the sandy areas. The Crown-of-Thorns starfish (which is known to feed on coral), is also a reef resident here, but its extent of predation on the corals is largely undetermined.

The outermost coral bar is a continuation of the north point of PUNTA LOS FRAILES, and extends almost the entire length of the bay, forming a submerged "barrier reef" that is actually broken up in a series of short, sandy stretches that alternate with the coral bars. Depths near the top of this coral bar average 25′ to 30′ (near PUNTA LOS FRAILES); and depths at its northernmost end (seaward of CABO PULMO) drop to 45′. The innermost coral reef begins in depths of 5′ and less at the southern end of Pulmo Bay and continues in a northeasterly direction toward PULMO POINT, reaching a depth of 20′. The middle reefs project in the same direction. Pulmo Bay is an open bay, and lacks protection from prevailing winds.

The CABO PULMO CORAL REEF, located over a shallow and easily accessible bay, is very fragile and highly susceptible to disturbances by man. The marine life in the area should be left undisturbed in their natural habitats, and divers should refrain from removing any of the coral or shell life in the area. Boaters who anchor over the reefs should take care not to destroy the coral with carelessly placed anchors.

OUTER PULMO REEF The outer Pulmo reef is located approximately 2 miles east of Cabo Pulmo Point. It is a submerged backbone ridge of large boulders, some reaching 20 feet in diameter, with the top of the ridge peaking within 20 foot of the surface. Depths around the ridge drop to 60′ and 70′ along a sandy ocean floor. Large caves and crevices along the ridge are lined with extremely varied and colorful gorgonian corals, sea fans, Tubastrae corals, and clumps of hard coral growths. The reef houses an abundance of interesting tropical reef species, including the beautiful longnose butterflyfish (Forcipiger flavissimus).

SHIPWRECKS There are two shipwrecks to explore in the Cabo Pulmo area. The first one, the wreck of the COLIMA, lies in 30' to 40' of water approximately 1-1/2 mile north of Cabo Pulmo Point. The wreck is strewn in several parts over a sandy ocean floor, and can be easily spotted in calm waters from the surface. An abundance of fish inhabit the wreck and photography is excellent. The ill-fated COLIMA was a large, Mexican freighter which was driven aground in a fierce storm in 1939.

The remains of a more recent shipwreck also lie approximately 1 mile northeast of Cabo Pulmo Point. A large Mexican tuna boat, about 90 feet long, sank in this area during a storm in 1978. The boat has been salvaged by locals, but the hull remains intact along the ocean floor in depths ranging from 40' to 60'. Silvery schools of bait fish swim over the hull of the boat, and larger snapper and grouper occupy its recesses. This shipwreck can also be easily spotted from the surface on a calm day of good water visibility, and local fishermen at the Cabo Pulmo settlement also frequently fish near the wreck.

Diving from small boats and inflatables is popular at Cabo Pulmo, where excellent diving reefs located just off shore are easily accessible.

NORTH FRAILES POINT comprises the southernmost point of PULMO BAY. It is accessible by boat from Los Frailes Bay or from the southern shore of Pulmo Bay. The prominent point is surrounded by large, detached rocks and boulders, with depths sloping quickly to 50' along a sandy ocean floor. Large submerged boulders are clustered around the easternmost portion of the point. Diving is good around the point, and snorkeling is also good in the shallows along the shoreline. Sculptured rock formations on the point create dramatic landscapes. Boat landings can be made on a small beach inside the point.

WHITE ROCK PINNACLE is located 500 yards north of NORTH FRAILES POINT, protruding above the surface of the water. This is an excellent diving location. The south side of the rock drops off almost vertically to depths of 80' and 90', ending in a sandy bottom. The north end of the rock forms the beginning of an underwater reef that continues northward from the rock, sloping gradually along its length to depths of 80'. Cabrilla, grouper, yellowtail, sierra, black sea bass, and even sea turtles frequent this isolated rock pinnacle.

LOS FRAILES (THE FRIAR'S ROCKS) are located midway down the length of FRAILES POINT. A small group of prominent detached rocks resembling praying monks, or friars, are responsible for the name of this area. These rock formations are accessible by boat only, and are usually inhabited by a small colony of sea lions. Depths slope gently from a rocky shoreline to 70'. Both snorkeling and diving in the area are excellent.

SOUTH FRAILES POINT forms the northern buttress of FRAILES BAY. A boat is the best access to the point, but it can be reached from the shoreline during low tide. Both snorkeling and diving are good around the point. Large boulders tumble to depths of 60' close in shore. Invertebrate life is not prolific, but schools of fish and tropical reef fish frequent the rocks. As the point continues westward toward the beach, depths become gradually shallower and rocks diminish in size.

LOS FRAILES BAY provides an excellent anchorage in prevailing northerly winds. Cruising yachts and sailboats frequent this scenic anchorage. Bottom depths within the bay reach 60', before converging with a deep submarine canyon that plunges to depths beyond the diver's reach. There is a beautiful beach back of the bay.

Punta Gorda to Land's End

Highway 1 closely parallels this southernmost portion of the coastline between the towns of San Jose del Cabo and Cabo San Lucas. The coastline is populated with resort hotels, condominiums and private residences, and encompasses some of the most beautiful stretches of beach and warmest waters in the Sea of Cortez. Snorkeling and diving are excellent around the numerous bays, coves and rocky points along the shoreline. Diving facilities are located in Cabo San Lucas, and diving trips can be arranged through most of the hotels.

PUNTA GORDA forms the northern end of the San Jose del Cabo Bay. A number of detached rocks fringe the point, where depths slope from 40' to 60' close around the point, then slope gradually seaward to depths over 100'. The point is a good diving location only in extremely calm weather. The point lacks protection from southerly wind conditions, and is often beset by surge and breakers. A dirt road leading east of San Jose del Cabo into a small fishing village provides the nearest land access to the point. Lobster and game fish are abundant around the point.

GORDA BANKS is a set of fishing banks which lie six miles east of PUNTA GORDA in the Sea of Cortez. It is not a practical sportdiving area, since the top of the inner set of banks generally rises to average depths within 90' to 100' of the surface. Open ocean conditions prevail, and currents, ocean swells and prevailing wind conditions combine with the extreme depths to create hazardous diving conditions. Only extremely experienced divers should descend upon these unprotected banks.

The submarine banks consist of a rocky submarine ridge thickly carpeted with invertebrate life and swarming with schools of reef and pelagic fish. GORDA BANKS are feeding grounds for large schools of tuna and jack, and also attract marlin, pelagic game fish, and sharks, including hammerheads, black tips, silver tips and tiger sharks, as well as the largest member of the shark family, the whale shark.

Whale sharks occur elsewhere in the Sea of Cortez, but they appear to frequent the Gorda Banks area in greater numbers in the springtime when the surface waters reach warmer temperatures. The local fishermen call these somnolent giants "Pez Sapo" (meaning

Diving in the Sea of Cortez can lead to such unexpected and exciting experiences as this unusual encounter with a whale shark, the largest fish in the ocean.

tadpole fish), as their shape is somewhat like a giant pollywog, with their round blunt heads and huge mouths nearly 6 feet across. Whale sharks appear to have no teeth, but actually have thousands of small teeth about 1/8″ long set in sheets around their jaws. The mouth acts like a great trawling net, straining tons of plankton, small sea life and schooling fish into its mouth.

Several sportdiving and filming expeditions have been able to observe the apparently docile nature of these giant beasts, who actually allow divers to swim right up to them and catch a ride on one of their dorsal or pectoral fins or on their back. Whale sharks actually seem totally unconcerned by the presence of divers. Even with divers on their backs, they continue their slow and somnolent cruising pace through the water, treating divers like any other hitchhiking remora.

Their seemingly languid pace, however, should not be equated with lack of strength or speed. Whale sharks are capable of sudden bursts of power which enable them to move through the water at extremely swift speeds. Whale sharks are the largest fish in the ocean, and can reach up to 80 feet in length. An underwater encounter with one of these mammoth creatures can only be described as a truly unforgettable experience.

PUNTA PALMILLA forms the southern point of San Jose del Cabo Bay, with a resort hotel perched atop its rocky bluff. A series of detached rocks form shallow reefs and tide pools around the point, with surge frequently breaking over them. Depths vary from 20' to 40' close to shore, providing good snorkeling and shallow diving on calm days. The beach curves south from HOTEL PALMILLA for several miles. It is characterized by low-lying rock outcroppings interspersed with stretches of clean, white sand.

PUERTO CHILENO is located 10 miles south of the San Jose del Cabo turnoff on Highway 1. The luxury resort of HOTEL CABO SAN LUCAS lies atop a rocky bluff overlooking the bay. Rocky shelves stretch several miles along the shoreline of Chileno Bay, forming a series of finger-like reefs which are honeycombed with crevices alive with invertebrate life and colorful reef fish. Tidepools along these reefs also teem with marine life. The underwater terrain ranges from shallow areas surrounding tide pools to rocky walls which drop to depths of 40' to 60' close around their base.

Easy beach entries can be made just south of the hotel to explore the reefs. Boats can also be launched 8 miles west at Cabo San Lucas to visit the cove, but attempts to anchor offshore along these reefs should only be done in fine weather.

SANTA MARIA COVE is a small, sheltered cove, well-protected in most wind conditions, lying just south of Puerto Chileno. A beautiful resort hotel, the TWIN DOLPHINS, lies just back of the cove. Snorkeling is good along both sides of the cove, in depths of 40' and less along rocky reefs and intervening sandy areas.

The north point of Santa Maria Cove reveals an underwater terrain dominated by large rocks, canyons, finger-like reefs and sandy channels running between the rock formations. Colorful gorgonians

PILOT WHALE
Globicephala macrorhynchus

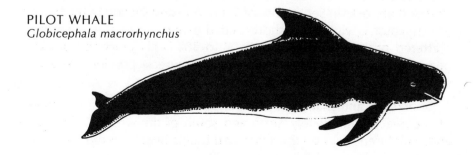

The remains of the Inari Manu Japanese freighter is a good shallow diving and snorkeling site.

and sea fans flourish along the rock walls, and fish life is abundant, with typical tropical reef fish.

The southern point around the cove is fringed with large rocks, underwater caverns and some coral outcroppings interspersed among the rocks. Lobsters and reef fish inhabit the rocks. Surge may break over the rocks in windy weather, creating poor diving conditions.

JAPANESE SHIPWRECK The Inari Maru No. 10 was wrecked and stranded on rocks in September of 1966. A rusted section of the hull of the freighter is visible on shore and the remains of the wreck are scattered offshore in depths from 5' to 30'. Easily reached from the beach or by boat, the remains of the wreck provide excellent snorkeling and shallow diving.

Snorkeling and shallow diving are possible along the entire length of the beach immediately north and south of the wreck. Tide pools and sculptured rocks on the shore add scenic beauty to the area.

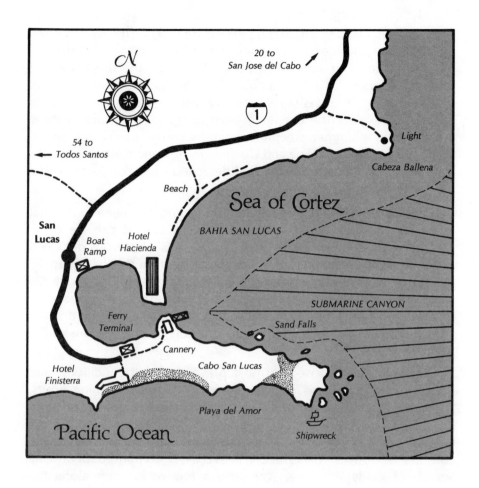

The map shows:

N (compass rose)

20 to San Jose del Cabo →

54 to Todos Santos ←

Light

Cabeza Ballena

1 (highway marker)

Beach

Sea of Cortez

San Lucas

Boat Ramp

Hotel Hacienda

BAHIA SAN LUCAS

SUBMARINE CANYON

Ferry Terminal

Sand Falls

Cannery

Cabo San Lucas

Hotel Finisterra

Playa del Amor

Pacific Ocean

Shipwreck

Cabo San Lucas

The picturesque granite pinnacles of CABO SAN LUCAS separate the pounding waters of the Pacific Ocean from the Sea of Cortez. They are very aptly named the "Land's End" pinnacles. Blue-green waters inside SAN LUCAS BAY are well-protected by the mighty granite cape, providing excellent conditions for sportdiving. A deep submarine trench closely following the configuration of the cove creates an unusual and breathtaking marine environment that attracts a great abundance of marine life. The famous underwater "SAND FALLS" of the submarine canyon are one of the area's most popular attractions for sportdivers.

CABO SAN LUCAS BAY has been declared an UNDERWATER PARK by Mexican authorities. No marine life may be removed from the Bay by sportdivers. The submarine trench has been the focal point of several scientific studies conducted by Scripps Institute of Oceanography in recent years. Only experienced divers should attempt to explore the deeper regions of the canyon, whose sheer granite walls plummet steeply to depths below the diver's reach. There are ample snorkeling and shallow diving opportunities in depths from 30' to 60' along the patches of detached rocks that lie along the arm of the Cape.

CABEZA BALLENA (Whale Head Point) is the prominent point that forms the northeastern point of San Lucas Bay. It can be easily recognized by the lighthouse atop its high cliffs. Numerous detached rocks surround the entire point. Depths range from shoal areas to 50' and 60' close around the point and continuing seaward for about 200 yards. The northernmost shoreline of CABEZA BALLENA reveals the greatest abundance of marine life, including reef fish, lobster, and the striped zebra moray eel, which is uncommon in other regions of the Sea of Cortez.

The point lies exposed to most prevailing wind conditions, and better diving conditions usually prevail during the morning hours. Snorkeling is good in the shallows, and visibility is excellent on calm days. There are few hazards in the area other than local winds, and this is a good diving location for divers of beginning and medium skills. The coastline southwest of CABEZA BALLENA is comprised of a long stretch of sandy shoreline, with only a few rocky reefs along the shoreline for snorkeling. The submarine canyon does not closely approach this side of the bay, and depths range from 30' to 40' as far as 150' yards offshore.

THE CANNERY AND PIER are located at the beginning of the rocky cape along the inside of San Lucas Bay. This locale provides an exciting diving location for avid fish photographers. As the cannery discharges fish offal into the water, schools of feeding fish converge around the pier in dense layers. A vertical food chain is formed, with the larger fish feeding upon schools of successively smaller fish.

Depths range from a shallow rocky shoreline to 30' and 40' along a sandy bottom, before joining the submarine canyon some 200 yards offshore. Boat traffic around the pier is a potential hazard for divers. Mullet, goatfish, yellowtail, sierra, jacks, roosterfish, grouper and other

The submarine canyon in San Lucas Bay approaches within 50 yards of shore, and is easily accessible from the beach.

large game fish congregate around the pier. The scattered remains of a large shipwreck protruding above the water from depths of 30' and less is located in the cove just east of the pier, and is a good snorkeling location.

DETACHED ROCK Midway down the arm of the Cape lying about 25 yards offshore is a large, detached flat-top granite rock. The submarine canyon closely approaches the rock on its northern side, and this is an excellent departure for descent into the submarine canyon. Depths around the rock slope from 20' on its shoreward side, gradually dropping to 60' on its seaward edge, then continuing steeply into the submarine canyon.

This small rocky pinnacle is thickly carpeted with invertebrate life, including orange Tubastrae corals, sea fans, indigo-colored gorgonians, and sea urchins. Tropical reef fish abound, including Moorish idols, parrotfish, sergeant majors and butterflyfish. This is an excellent night diving location in calm weather, as small boats can be easily anchored near the rock. At night, thick carpets of orange, Tubastrea corals covering the rock surfaces open their delicate, flower-like polyps to feed in the currents.

PLAYA DEL AMOR (Lover's Beach) It is only fitting that one of the most beautiful beaches in Baja should be located on a magnificently sculptured ridge of granite separating two mighty bodies of water, whose waves wash up on both sides of this beach. On its northern shore, this lovely beach faces the tranquil and emerald-green waters of the SAN LUCAS BAY, the southernmost bay in the Sea of Cortez. Small boats can anchor just off the beach on calm days. This beach faces the submarine canyon, which approaches within 50 yards of its shoreline, and is an excellent place to conduct beach diving activities into the canyon. Its southern shore opens up onto a vast expanse of sandy beach that is washed by the pounding surf of the Pacific Ocean.

SHEPHERD'S ROCK is the detached knife-like pinnacle that comes into prominent view east of PLAYA DEL AMOR. It is covered with white bird lime, and rises 25 feet above the surface. Immediate depths around the rock are shallow, from 20' to 30', with similar submerged rocks nearby. Shephard's Rock is barren and surrounded by sand, and though of little interest by itself for divers or photographers, it marks one of the best points of departure from which to descend into the submarine canyon to explore the canyon walls and the submarine "sand falls," which lie just northwest of the base of the pinnacle.

SUBMARINE CANYON The continental shelves along California and Baja California are slashed with deep gorges and canyons, but none is more spectacular than the jagged submarine trench that drops almost vertically down to abyssal depths in the SAN LUCAS BAY. The upper shelf of the canyon is covered with coarse sand, which extends from the beach and continues underwater over the rim of the canyon, forming steep sandy slopes down to depths of 50'–80'. Below this, rock outcrops begin to protrude above the sand. They become gradually more dense, finally giving way to steep, vertical granite walls and rocky ledges at a depth of about 100'.

As the coarse sand continues into the canyon from the rim it is channeled in between steep rocky canyons, and slowly flows downward like a broad river on land. At depths of 130' to 150', these rivers of sand are constricted into narrower and narrower channels, and their flow becomes more vigorous. Deeper still, these rivers of sand finally cascade over the sheer walls of the canyon, looking very much like waterfalls. An expedition from Scripps Institute of Oceanography in 1960 first photographed the movement of the rivers of sand flowing into the submarine canyon, and dubbed them "sand falls."

A diver peers over one of the narrow rivers of sand that cascades into the deep submarine canyon.

The submarine precipices of the canyon are softened by thick growths of gorgonian corals and sea fans appearing in a variety of colors and forms. Tropical reef fish thrive along the rocky ledges, and Indo-Pacific fish species (fish life characteristic of Indian Ocean and Pacific Ocean tropical islands) are especially dominant. Schools of barracuda and other pelagic game fish also feed in the rich and fertile current-fed depths of the canyon.

LAND'S END The tip of the Baja California peninsula terminates abruptly in a magnificent vaulting natural arch, known as "land's end." Slightly seaward lie two solitary granite pinnacles well over 200 feet high that stand as mighty sentinels guarding the entrance to the Sea of Cortez. These colossal chunks of granite mark the point at which the waters of the Pacific converge with the Sea of Cortez.

A colony of sea lions inhabits these rock pinnacles, whose steep and barren submarine walls plummet to a sandy bottom with depths at their bases ranging from 30' to 80'. The easternmost rocky pinnacle protrudes 10' above the water, and is a good diving location on calm days, with depths around it reaching 80' and continuing into the submarine canyon. Severe currents can arise quickly around the point, however, and surge from Pacific Ocean swells can make diving conditions in this area hazardous.

SUNKEN SHIP The remains of a wrecked freighter lie in 50' of water, approximately 75 yards southwest of the granite rocks at the tip of the Cape. Located in Pacific Ocean waters, the wreck has been largely scattered by surge and waves, but portions of it still remain intact along the sandy bottom, offering good sightseeing and photography when diving conditions are favorable.

Fish Identification Index

Some common fish species that divers are likely to see around reefs in the Sea of Cortez have been included in this section. They are indexed below for quick reference by their photo numbers as they appear on the following pages, and are grouped by families.

PHOTO CREDITS: Photos #6, 9, 11, 28, 36, 37, 39, 40, 47, 50, 54, 55, 56, 59, and 63 taken by Howard Hall; Photos #3, 5, 7, 12, 14, and 53 taken by Marty Snyderman; all other photos taken by the authors.

ANGELFISH

Cortez Angelfish - photo #4
King Angelfish - photo #2
Clarion Angelfish - photo #40

BASS

Barred Serrano - photo #12
Spotted Sand Bass - photo #11
Leather Bass - photo #13
Panama Graysby - photo #48
Flag Cabrilla - photo #50
Spotted Cabrilla - photo #9
Leopard Grouper - photo #46
Golden Grouper - photo #15
Pacific Creolefish - photo #32

BUTTERFLYFISH

Threebanded Butterflyfish - photo #58
Barberfish - photo #7
Longnose Butterflyfish - photo #1

DAMSELFISH

Scissortail Damselfish - photo #52
Giant Damselfish - photo #6
Cortez Damselfish (juvenile) - photo #55

Sergeant Major - photos #42 & #44
Blue-and-yellow Chromis - photo #45

HAWKFISHES

Coral Hawkfish - photo #31
Giant Hawkfish - photo #53

JAWFISH; BLENNIES; GOBIES

Redhead Goby - photo #21
Lizard Triplefin - photo #14
Bluespotted Jawfish - photo #10

PARROTFISH

Azure Parrotfish photos #17 & #18
Bluechin Parrotfish - photos #16 & #23

PUFFERFISH; PORCUPINEFISH

Guineafowl Puffer - photo #43
Golden Puffer - photo #47
Spotted Sharpnose Puffer - photo #56
Porcupinefish - photos #41 & #57

SNAPPERS; GRUNTS; PORGIES

Dog Snapper - photo #64
Barred Pargo - photo #27
Yellow Snapper - photo #35
Blue and Gold Snapper -
    photo #37
Garybar Grunt - photo #36
Wavyline Grunt - photo #29
Panamic Porkfish - photo #38
Pacific Porgy - photo #39

TRIGGERFISH
Balistidae

Finescale Triggerfish -
    photo #60
Blunthead Triggerfish -
    photo #8
Orangeside Triggerfish -
    photo #54

WRASSES
Labridae

Mexican Hogfish - photos
#49 & #59

California Sheephead -
    photo #51
Cortez Rainbow Wrasse -
    photos #61 & #62
Sunset Wrasse - photo #22

OTHER REEF FISH

Barspot Cardinalfish -
    photo #28
Mexican Goatfish - photo #30
Moorish Idol - photo #26
Panamic Soldierfish - photo #19
Reef Cornetfish - photo #20
Stone Scorpionfish - photo #3
Yellowtail Surgeonfish -
    photo #5

PELAGIC FISH

Almaco Amberjack - photo #25
Crevalle Jack - photo #34
Gafftopsail Pompano -
    photo #33
Mexican Barracuda - photo #24
Yellowtail - photo #63

1. Longnose Butterflyfish

2. King Angelfish

3. Stone Scorpionfish

4. Cortez Angelfish

5. Yellowtail Surgeonfish

6. Giant Damselfish

7. Barberfish

8. Blunthead triggerfish

9. Spotted Cabrilla

10. Bluespotted Jawfish

11. Spotted Sand Bass

12. Barred Serrano

13. Leather Bass

14. Lizard Triplefin

15. Golden Grouper

16. Bluechin Parrotfish

17. Azure Parrotfish (female)

18. Azure Parrotfish (male)

19. Panamic Soldierfish

20. Reef Cornetfish

21. Redhead Goby

22. Sunset Wrasse (adult)

23. Bluechin parrotfish (female)

24. Mexican Barracuda

25. Almaco Amberjack

26. Moorish Idol

27. Barred Pargo

28. Barspot Cardinalfish

29. Wavyline Grunt

30. Mexican Goatfish

31. Coral Hawkfish

32. Pacific Creolefish

33. Gafftopsail Pompano

34. Crevalle Jack

35. Yellow Snapper

36. Graybar Grunt

37. Blue-and-Gold Snapper

38. Panamic Porkfish

39. Pacific Porgy

40. Clarion Angelfish

41. Spotted Porcupinefish

42. Panamic Sergeant Major
(normal adult color)

43. Guineafowl Puffer

44. Panamic Sergeant Major
(breeding male)

45. Blue-and-Yellow Chromis

46. Leopard Grouper

47. Guineafowl Puffer
(beginning golden phase)

48. Panama Graysby

49. Mexican Hogfish (female)

50. Flag Cabrilla

51. California Sheephead

52. Scissortail Damselfish

53. Giant Hawkfish

54. Orangeside Triggerfish

55. Cortez Damselfish (juvenile)

56. Spotted Sharpnose Puffer

57. Porcupinefish (also: Balloonfish)

58. Three-banded Butterflyfish

59. Mexican Hogfish (male)

60. Finescale Triggerfish

61. Cortez Rainbow Wrasse

62. Cortez Rainbow Wrasse
(upper: male)

63. Yellowtail

64. Pacific Dog Snapper

Index